A Rhetoric of Pleasure

Prose Style and Today's Composition Classroom

T. R. Johnson

New Perspectives in Rhetoric and Composition

CHARLES I. SCHUSTER, SERIES EDITOR

Boynton/Cook Publishers
HEINEMANN
Portsmouth, NH

Boynton/Cook Publishers, Inc.
A subsidiary of Reed Elsevier Inc.
361 Hanover Street
Portsmouth, NH 03801-3912
www.boyntoncook.com

Offices and agents throughout the world

Library of Congress Cataloging-in-Publication Data
Johnson, T. R., 1964–
    A rhetoric of pleasure : prose style and today's composition classroom /
    T. R. Johnson.
      p. cm.
    Includes bibliographical references.
    ISBN 0-86709-526-1 (alk. paper)
    1. English language—Rhetoric—Study and teaching. 2. English
language—Style—Study and teaching. 3. Report writing—Study and
teaching (Higher).   I. Title.

PE1404.J65 2003
808'.042'0711—dc21   2002155264

Editor: Charles I. Schuster
Production: Vicki Kasabian
Cover design: Joni Doherty
Typesetter: TechBooks, Inc.
Manufacturing: Steve Bernier

Printed in the United States of America on acid-free paper
07 06 05 04 03 DA 1 2 3 4 5

Contents

Acknowledgments

I wrote this book for my students, my teachers, and also my friends, among them: Gary Anderson, Dale Ashmun, Michele Baker, Emily Bingham, Lynn Birkett, Ethan Buckler, Tom Byers, Lisa Carver, John Cooke, Marylin Cooper, Susan Danielson, George Daul, Christine Day, Leon Driscoll, Chris Dunn, Liz Durham-Foye, Nancy Easterlin, Scott Farrin, Ricky Feather, Brian Foye, David Grubbs, John Hazlett, Todd Harper, David Helm, Suzette Henke, Eric and Nichole Houghton, Marla Humphress, Chris Iovenko, Brian Johnson, Ed Johnson, Mike Jones, Sally Kaylor, Kris Lackey, both Kathleen Lyonses, Harold Maier, Rebecca Matheny, Michael Meese, Leslie Millar, Hildy Miller, Robert Nedelkoff, Bonnie Noonan, Tom Pace, Matt Parfitt, Sondra Perl, Brett Ralph, Ken Rayes, Michael Relish, Donice Reiss, Dora Rice, Mary Ruetten, Bob Shenk, Richard Schuler, Charles Schuster, Dawn Skorczewski, Bob Sturges, Britt Walford, Willy Walsh, Rachel Weathers, Les White, Joyce Zonana, my two brothers, Clark and Ben, their families, and, above all, my parents, Julie and Dick.

Introduction

The recent shootings at schools in Alaska, Arkansas, California, Colorado, Florida, Kentucky, Mississippi, Oregon, Pennsylvania, and Washington have summoned a curious chain of memories of my days in elementary school, memories that return to me more and more these days as I reflect on my practice as a teacher of writing. In the earliest memory, I am standing at the bottom of the steps in front of my school with several dozen other kids, looking around for pals from my neighborhood with whom I would walk home. We are all thrilling to the strong sunlight of the Louisville autumn afternoon, when suddenly an older, bigger kid comes crashing through the crowd. Before disappearing around the corner, he pauses and cries out,

> *School's out—ring the bell!*
> *Drop your books—run like hell!*

I immediately laughed, for in those days, the only thing funnier than profane language was profane language that rhymed. The jingle did what all jingles do—it stuck in my head, where, more than twenty-five years later, it still jingles. Over the next few weeks, I often repeated the rhyme, and my audience always greeted it with laughter. I remember sharing the couplet near the end of the school year, when it had a particular charm, with some kids who were casually practicing their jump shots on the basketball courts behind my parents' house. As expected, they all laughed. One of them, though, did me one better. "Listen to this," he said,

> *No more chalkboards! No more chairs!*
> *Throw the teachers down the stairs!*

We all roared, but our laughter was mirthless and mean. Though lacking profanity, the rhyme flared with a special appeal, a special rancor and rowdiness, for it targeted the teachers for physical violence.

We were not particularly rough kids. No one ever brought a knife, much less a gun, to school. I feel fairly certain—though I can't know for sure—that none of us was any more interested in turning a gun on our teachers or classmates than our rhymes were incantations from satanic ritual or ur-texts for the gangsta rap of the decades that would follow. On the other hand, I can't help but wonder if the horrifying violence

v

now synonymous with Columbine isn't more properly understood as somehow pervasive.[1] What leads me to consider this possibility is my memory of a third rhyme, one that was vastly more popular than the first two and, in the context of Columbine, vastly more disturbing.

Next to the basketball court where I had learned the second one, a youth group had installed, through the sponsorship of a nearby Catholic church, a trailer and decked it out with a stereo, strobe lights, shag rug, bean-bag chairs, and posters of rock stars. Although I was too young at the time to have more than a dim idea of what went on in the trailer, my parents made it clear that under no circumstances was I to go anywhere near it. And so, as often as possible, I did. I never went inside, though, because the kids who ran it had a rule that you had to be at least thirteen to enter. Long before I reached thirteen, the youth group's clubhouse was shut down, for it had quickly become a font of values that were—to put it mildly—incommensurate with those of its sponsor. But, during its brief tenure, I would hang around in front of the place, try to be invisible, and learn as much as I dared. It was here that I learned the rhyme that thoroughly outstripped the others.

Early one Saturday evening, before I was called home, I was tossing a football back and forth nearby with my younger brother. We were both transfixed by two girls who were smoking cigarettes on the steps in front of the trailer. I recall that the girls were singing all sorts of songs that evening, but only one stands out in my memory. I'm certain that I'll never forget it. The tune was "The Battle Hymn of the Republic," but the words weren't. Here they are:

> *Glory, glory allelujah*
> *The teacher hit me with a ruler,*
> *So I met her at the gate*
> *With a loaded .38*
> *And there ain't no teacher no more!*

They laughed, and then continued:

> *My eyes have seen the glory*
> *Of the burning of the school!*
> *We have tortured every teacher!*
> *We have broken every rule!*
> *We have crucified the principal*
> *And hung him on the wall—*
> *Our truth goes marching on!*

My brother and I stared at each other, wide-eyed. We had no idea what to think or say or feel. I only knew that I would never have to bother memorizing these lines, for they were instantly a part of me.

Murder, arson, anarchy, and sadism: these are certainly no nursery rhymes. But their general logic follows directly out of the earlier pair. They all three give voice to a powerful rancor, a supremely negative reaction against the experience of being in school. I'm certain that the girls were just playing around, cracking themselves up by repeating what somebody had repeated to them the week before. During my middle-school years, I too would repeat these rhymes all the time, and I'm sure the kids who heard me did the same. These awful little verses flew through Louisville's pre-teen world in the mid-70s until seemingly every student I knew had heard them, and, as far as I know, they're still making the rounds among that age group. In other words, while only a tiny percentage of students begin to drift toward the interpersonal free-fall of the Trenchcoat Mafia and its analogues, the overwhelming majority take an obvious delight in apocalyptic images of their own aggression against their school and its authorities.

But why? Where does such rancor—however playfully expressed—come from? How does it manifest itself within the processes of learning how to write? What form does it take among students at the college level? Part of the difficulty of answering these questions is their sheer banality. As Bart Simpson or Beavis or Butthead or any of the denizens of *Wayne's World* or *South Park* would put it, "School sucks." Everybody knows this. But how does this attitude impact the way students inhabit the composing process and the ways they come to engage the symbolic field of their culture? And how can we differentiate the sort of anger that fuels the critical thinking that schools so prize from the Beavis and Butthead variety of the rhymes I used to repeat all the time?

None of these questions will allow for simple, conclusive answers. I want especially to resist the idea that we can rig up an interpretation of the terror at Columbine that will serve in a general way to illuminate all student experience. The link, in other words, between Columbine and those vicious schoolyard rhymes is tenuous at best; the popularity of those rhymes probably owes more to their cleverness and general air of scandal than to any omnipresent if subterranean appetite for meticulously plotted slaughter. Nonetheless, the link, however limited, seems worth pondering—at least as a starting point for broader inquiry into the ways our students experience our pedagogy.

Yet another difficulty in exploring these questions, however, is the relative absence of any discussion of them in the history of composition studies. One might turn to our discourse about students' resistance to our pedagogies, but "resistance" seems far too mild a word for the massacres—both actual and fantasized—that occasion my thinking here. Besides, our field borrowed the concept of resistance from psychoanalysts, for whom the term designates a certain repressive refusal of the truths of unconscious desire as they threaten to manifest themselves during the process of analysis. Again, "resistance" is hardly the word for what is not, after all, a pattern of repression but an explosion of rage.

Because our field has so little precedent for approaching this terrain directly, I would like to approach it through its opposite—that is, through what we know about how students *take pleasure in learning to write*. For here, we do have at least a few clues, some inklings, some slightly more familiar ground. Perhaps by delineating this terrain, we can then manage to turn it upside-down or inside-out to abstract a tentative, skeletal outline of student rage. More precisely, if we can pin down what authorial pleasure is, we can then suppose that this assemblage of possibilities is what many students can't seem to access; we can then think about why and what we might do to make the pleasures of writing more available to them.

After all, learning to write is by no means *always* a dreadful experience. On innumerable occasions, when I've halted class discussion and asked the students to scribble down their thoughts or begin drafting an essay, I've invariably seen at least a few of them, after a minute or two, register that strange, highly positive surge of energy—and their pens begin to wiggle across the page more quickly than a moment before, their heads lower a notch, and they emanate a whole new kind of intensity. Intuitively, I sense that the stuff they write while in this experiential mode is more engaged and engaging than the other stuff, which in comparison comes to feel like a mere warm-up. Their writing is full of an energy that, I've always assumed, comes from opening onto the raw flow of the composing process and from engaging the particulars of the immediate context. They are sparked by the lively oral exchange that immediately preceded their writing, and, just as anyone's remarks in that exchange could be retracted or critiqued or contradicted by anyone else, students seem to write in these inspired moments with a flexibility, an openness to revision that generally does not characterize the writing they do as homework. Instead of knocking out a perfunctory exercise or simply parroting what they think I want to hear, many of them seem to be growing and changing before my eyes, reversing the alienation that had held their minds in check, becoming other than what they were. When this happens, I find myself feeling that something vaguely miraculous is afoot, that the long-standing tradition that links rhetoric to magic is, despite its problems from a professional point of view, worth thinking about.

Indeed, I've devoted this book to exploring that moment. For, not only do we know very little about it, what little we do know is riddled with incommensurable half-truths that can only scuttle our attempts to make it available to students. More specifically, most of us want, on one hand, to lead our students to take pleasure in the composing process, so they will work harder at it and continue to cultivate rhetorical skill long after they've left our classrooms. On the other hand, we're suspicious of such pleasure because we associate it with sheer whimsy and self-indulgence and because we assume that it necessarily gets in the way of teaching and learning the public conventions that enable clear, communicative prose. Thus, we enter our classrooms, day after day, with a contradictory sense of mission and a sharply diminished chance of succeeding. For a generation or so, we have valorized a rigorous awareness of convention and audience—the disciplined writer—and we've done so quite possibly because we've sought to ensure the disciplinary status of composition itself. But even before this emphasis emerged, we produced virtually no research whatsoever on the pleasure of composing, because, as one teacher put it, "it's squishy, it's difficult to predict, and talking about it seems vaguely unprofessional."[2]

And yet certain questions continue to haunt our classrooms. What is authorial pleasure? What role does it play in becoming a better writer? How, at the level of daily practice, might a better understanding of it take us beyond the tentative, intuitive gestures by which we aim to maintain a positive classroom "atmosphere"? When we bury these concerns with the claims that they are unavailable to theoretical, historical, and empirical inquiry, and that they are opposed to the more important questions of how to teach an awareness of convention, correctness, and audience, we make for them, at best, an unquiet grave and open the way for their constant, uncanny return.

This book celebrates that return by showing how authorial pleasure is concretely linked—rather than hazily opposed—to the sorts of rigor and clarity prized in well-disciplined, professional discourse; how pleasure's link to clarity and persuasion has sparked some 2,500 years of inquiry into its precise nature and importance; and thus how authorial pleasure is therefore an entirely legitimate, even crucial concern for the teacher of writing today.

A Rhetoric of Pleasure, on one hand, is perhaps not the very best place for someone wholly new to the field of composition to begin reading about how to teach writing, for it will engage the thinking of an admittedly wild array of figures—Antiphon, Baudrillard, Blake, Cixous, Deleuze, Gorgias, Lacan, Longinus, Zizek—and it will use their ideas to dialogue with the equally diverse array of figures who have led the field of composition theory through the last thirty years. On the other hand, however, this book is also filled with the voices of actual students, and thus anyone who has spent time in the classroom will quickly recognize the situations and concerns this book addresses. *A Rhetoric of Pleasure* ultimately seeks to provide an intellectual framework that can help experienced teachers reflect more and more deliberately on the sorts of problems that, at least intuitively if not consciously, arise constantly in their day-to-day teaching. At the same time, it hopes to introduce relative newcomers to the profession of composition to rich traditions of debate that have long preceded their arrival and that will likely continue for many generations to come.

Those who train graduate students to teach, as well as those who administer writing programs, writing-across-the-curriculum programs, or writing centers, will find here a fund of resources that is explicitly designed to help them have very productive, even unifying conversations with academic factions most often at odds with each other: say, deans in colleges of business or engineering who aren't inclined to budge from the imperative of getting students to communicate more efficiently, and the gender radicals and avant-garde poets whose ultimate concerns are often elsewhere. In fact, this book seeks to help composition administrators negotiate productive resolutions, even ongoing conversations between such potential antagonists (golfers versus goddess-worshippers), and it will do so by defining authorial pleasure through a tradition of complex reflection on matters of style and desire in the writing classroom.

In short, this book weds a sympathy for the most radical moments in Western thought with the routine, workaday mandate to get students to write more "clearly." Thus, *A Rhetoric of Pleasure* calls for no sweeping reforms in the goals of even the most hoary and hidebound programs in writing instruction; instead, it calls for quite radical reforms in the ways we have traditionally *understood* these goals, so that we can accomplish them more often and stave off the more regrettable possibilities that can derive from this dominant paradigm.

What motivated me the most in writing this book, however, was simply a concern for today's students. I believe our students are facing the challenge of learning how to write at a particularly difficult, even alienating moment in our institutional history. In fact, I'll even claim that I'm offering this book at a dire phase in the evolution of composition studies. We've heard so much talk lately about the vertiginous fragmenting and cross-fertilization within the old disciplinary machinery of the humanities, so many questions about what "discipline" might mean and whether or not composition is a discipline (or perhaps more than one) and what the stakes are, that I fear that what seems most professional and legitimating and thus at a premium during these chaotic times is *pain,* the pain we can inflict on each other and on those least able to fight back, our students. After all, if pleasure is "squishy" and unprofessional, then what might seem most professional and legitimating during this interval of instability and change is pain. Indeed, wherever there are destabilized belief systems and deeply challenged institutional self-conceptions, as Elaine Scarry notes, whenever the ordering mechanisms of a population come to seem unreal or arbitrary, people will seek to assuage the anxiety that results from these circumstances by reinscribing and re-anchoring these structures in ways that will make them most immediately real and most immediately felt. That is, people will proceed—on behalf of these structures—with the dirty work of inflicting pain.

Surely, when a teacher of writing pushes a too-rigorous suspicion of authorial pleasure in the name of convention-based writing (whatever that might mean), some students will come to see the academy as an alien monolith, an infernal machine so intimidating that they succumb to a nervousness that altogether undermines their ability to write. And everyone knows of a graduate student who became trapped inside an interfaculty grudge match and failed to survive professionally. I fear that we take responsibility for such casualties only the way that an obscure terrorist sect might: not as symptoms of our confusion, but as proof of the seriousness of our own individual agenda and as a means to bolster our own claims to authority.

Such a sorrowful phenomenon is, of course, by no means entirely new, not purely a function of the recent blurring of disciplinary boundaries. Ever since Plato banished the poets from his ideal republic and blasted the sophists for trafficking in a similar brand of ecstatic make-believe, the academy has frowned upon pleasure as an "unprofessional" consideration. Over the last decade or two, however, I fear that our frowns have deepened and, as a kind of signature, they've taken a second meaning: as we come to see that the price of professional and disciplinary status is pleasure, we can't help but worry about how we'll attract new generations to our field; how we'll manage to make significant, positive impressions on our students; how, in fact, we'll manage to do anything but perpetuate ourselves a short while as a dreary bureaucracy of banal abstraction.

Indeed, I've often encountered colleagues in the field of rhetoric and composition who insist that the topic of authorial pleasure is wholly irrelevant to our field, and, what's more, that they have never enjoyed writing at all and don't encourage their students to think of writing in terms of enjoyment. Such moments are invariably disorienting, something like hearing astronauts declare that they don't like to fly. I can't help but feel saddened, too, by such assertions: why the refusal of all question of the lived experience of writing? What horrors lurk there? Can't one expect that, like a bad penny, the question of the quality of one's experience will return again and again? Might not a good strategy be to welcome this question, to engage it with genuine rigor, to let it focus our critical thinking, and ultimately to allow it to drive our writing and teaching? If our goal, at least partly, is to empower our writing students, how can we refuse to discuss the experience of such empowerment, the experience of authorial pleasure? To continue in this refusal is to risk turning our students into those sad people who must tell themselves, over and over, that their pleasure doesn't really matter, that experience isn't all that interesting or important, the kind of astronauts who really can't bear to leave the ground.

This book has one primary purpose: to define authorial pleasure through a long but "renegade" tradition in the history of rhetoric *not* as the stuff of whimsical self-indulgence but as a feeling of connection with one's audience. Toward that end, I borrow particular moments in the history of rhetoric in order to construct something like a tradition of pleasure-oriented pedagogy, and I juxtapose that tradition with accounts of my own classroom and excerpts from my students' papers, ultimately to describe a composition classroom that takes authorial pleasure seriously. If, in recent decades, we have strenuously disavowed this sort of renegade terrain in order to ascend to positions of authority and privilege within the university, perhaps the time has come, given our relative success in establishing ourselves, to reclaim some of the more radical possibilities of the legacy we inherit.

Chapter 1 explores the problem of trying to imagine a contemporary writing course that takes pleasure seriously. It sketches how theories of rhetoric that entertain such a possibility have historically run afoul of the practical demands of the academic institution. This first chapter pays particular attention to recent decades in which the field of composition has become professionalized and a postmodern, consumer culture has diminished, even "perverted" the potential for authorial pleasure in today's classroom. This first chapter, however, will also recount a particular classroom activity I tried a few years ago that enabled a quite different, quite significant sort of pleasure in my students.

Chapter 2 describes how I recently expanded that activity in a first-year composition class. This chapter begins by discussing particular shortcomings in the dominant approaches to writing instruction of recent decades—expressivism and social constructionism—and, specifically, how their respective interests in voice and discourse fall short on the subject of authorial pleasure and its role in learning to write. After delineating my dissatisfaction with these approaches, I sketch in this chapter a contrasting set of ideas culled from what we know about the rhapsodes of preclassical Greece and the sophists who followed them. These ideas have allowed me to set aside concepts of voice and discourse to develop a pedagogy based on the transpersonal power of sound. This pedagogy, which I describe in the remainder of the chapter, shows students how to use this power by playing around, quite pleasurably, with devices and principles of prose style.

Chapter 3 documents my students' responses to this style-based pedagogy. More specifically, it juxtaposes excerpts from the writing my students gave me on the last day of the semester with versions of that "renegade" tradition in the history of rhetoric that addresses matters of authorial pleasure. I suggest that these ancient and much-marginalized ideas are still floating around our culture at the level of intuition and the most grassroots sort of lore. First, however, I create a helpful context for these connections between my students' remarks and these relatively remote and exotic theories of rhetoric by returning to matters first mentioned here in the introduction and developed in the first chapter: the possibility that the contemporary social landscape is a source of acute, even life-defining displeasure among our students. For only in this context can I make much sense of why my students would echo so strongly ideas first set forth by those thinkers who directly inherited the traditions of the rhapsodes and sophists—this is, by the Hellenistic school, and, in particular, the Stoics. These thinkers centralize the same point that arose most conspicuously in my students' final papers: that carefully stylized writing isn't merely fun, but that its pleasures can play an essential role in personal transformation, even healing.

Chapter 4 traces yet more directly the ways this ancient tradition can reach into the contemporary classroom and focuses, in particular, on what many in composition would likely assume is a primary problem with pleasure-based pedagogies. The problem with these pedagogies is that they simply don't give the teacher enough to do and thereby threaten the seriousness, the dignity, and the authority of the teacher of writing within the larger context of the academy. This final chapter then concludes by explaining the role of the teacher in the pleasure-based pedagogy I advocate and delineating the particular responsibilities and rigors that are essential to his or her moment to practice in the classroom. This final chapter therefore ends by bringing the book full circle to the conflict first set forth in Chapter 1 between pleasure and professionalism.

In sum, this book examines the way a style-based approach to teaching composition can simultaneously help students to write more effectively *and* find in their writing a significant, even therapeutic pleasure. By contextualizing this approach in a centuries-old discussion of the experience of authorial pleasure, one that in recent decades we have obscured and sacrificed at considerable expense to our students, this book hopes to elucidate and dignify the student writer's potential for composing pleasure.

Notes

1. At the risk of eliding important details and forgetting incidents that must never be forgotten, I'd like the word "Columbine" to serve in this book as a kind of grim shorthand for all of the other catastrophic episodes of school violence that have come to occur with such dread frequency in the last five years.

2. These are the words of Lex Runciman (1991). Many in composition have echoed Runciman's frustration with our reluctance to discuss pleasure. As Richard Fulkerson recently noted, we have seen through the mid-'90s a sort of mini-groundswell in works that address the affective domain, from traditional cognitivist and expressivist studies to those that embrace a more expansive, spiritualized agenda to those informed by postmodern and Lacanian discourses. None of these, however, move us beyond the deadlocked Elbow-Bartholomae debate of 1995, for none of them grapple with the ways a concern for pleasure would seem to run counter to the sorts of rigors necessary to cultivate our fledgling disciplinarity.

One

"School Sucks"

Sacred incantations sung with words are bearers of pleasure and banishers of pain, for . . . the power of incantation is wont to beguile [the soul] and persuade it and alter it by witchcraft . . . [one can] come under the influence of [a] speech just as if ravished by the force of the mighty.

—Gorgias, circa 414 B.C.E.

Pedagogy *refers to the power to impose meanings that maintain and reinforce the reigning social, economic, and political arrangements as legitimate when they are in fact entirely arbitrary . . . . Dominant pedagogy is a structure that produces individuals and groups who are recognized as such because they have internalized the legitimate point of view. Pedagogy retains its authority precisely through violence, through its power to impose the legitimate mode of conception and perception, through its power to conceal and mystify relations of power and domination . . . . Dominant pedagogy depends on the social misrecognition of the objective truth of pedagogic work. (221)*

—Lynn Worsham, 1998

For as long as people have tried to think about writing and how to teach it, they have thought too about the pleasures involved in rhetorical activity. Some twenty-five-hundred years ago, Gorgias put pleasure, as we see in the first epigraph above, at the center of his theory of rhetoric. The experience Gorgias identifies here probably derives from what Walter Ong calls the "psychodynamics of orality"— that is, from the particular epistemology and rhetorical practices of pre-literate culture. In cultures without writing, such as the one that

1

immediately preceded the classical world, all knowledge takes the form of easily remembered incantations and chants that can induce not merely an experience of collectivity, but a sort of rhapsodic, ecstatic, Dionysian dissolution into the pulsing energy of the crowd (Ong 1982, 45–46; Dodds 1951, 76–79; Davis 2000, 26–30).

This transformative power implicit in oralist discourse initially served Gorgias and other sophists as the principal force to be harnessed in a medical or therapeutic language practice: for "words," as Gorgias says, "are bearers of pleasure and banishers of pain." Because illness was understood as a mark against one's moral character, a punishment for some infraction that alienated the sufferer from the community, the skilled rhetorical healer, according to Pedro Lain Entralgo (1970), sought to change the meaning of this alienating mark by wrapping it in a new verbal context—that is, by juxtaposing it with sacred songs and healing chants (40–41). The rhetor released the patient from the stigmatized personae in which he or she had been trapped and freed the patient to pursue states of increased well-being and increasingly energetic, even Dionysian, reimmersion in the community.

This therapeutic practice, Entralgo further suggests, eventually became the model for how persuasion works. In short, the rhetorical work of transforming a suffering patient from a state of illness to one of comparative comfort and well-being became the prototype for transforming an audience from one opinion or point of view to another. For Gorgias, the work of persuading an audience, like the work of alleviating suffering, hinged upon creating in the audience an experience of well-being, an experience of aesthetic pleasure or "terpsis." For, once the rhetor had stimulated in the listeners a state of rapt attention and openness to change, they were more easily swayed in the direction the rhetor wanted them to go. Rhetors generated this all-important pleasure in the audience, first, by making sure that it emanated from themselves during their own rhetorical performances. It could then spread contagiously to the audience, repeating and redoubling itself among them (Segal 1962, 126).

Gorgias' theory applies in a very direct and commonsensical way to our own classrooms: before students can learn how to persuade an audience of anything, the student must first learn to experience composing itself as a kind of pleasure-charged performance, for once they learn to generate a rigorous, positive excitement around the task of rhetorical action, they'll stand a much greater chance of spreading that feeling to their audience. In fact, we can formulate from Gorgias a working definition of authorial pleasure: it is the feeling that ensues during the composing process that is roughly analogous to the transformation of pain and alienation into knowledge and connection, and its contagious quality is the stuff of persuasion, perhaps of communication.

But what is most troubling about Gorgias' theory—and thoroughly crippling for teachers of today who would base their pedagogies upon it—is that he explicitly understands the contagion of pleasure in terms of magical spells and witchcraft. And this occult motif persists wherever the issue of pleasure arises throughout the history of rhetoric. For example, when Marsilio Ficino published *Da Vita* in the late 1400s, he explicitly identified the topic of his book as ecstasy, and he proceeded to load his book with what we would today identify as astrology. Ficino insists that he is not simply encouraging people to worship stars, but to use the stars as a subsidiary symbol-system by which to organize the natural potential for ecstasy in speech and songs (Ficino 1989, 357, 363). Ficino casts the constantly shifting heavenly bodies as symbols to be used in keeping track of ever-shifting rhetorical contexts, and, as such, the stars were essential tools in the heady intertwining of "process" and "context" by which Ficino sought to accomplish his overall project of living joyfully. But the fact that Ficino linked the pleasure of rhetorical activity to magic, as Gorgias did, made him vulnerable to attack from mainstream, rationalist intellectuals of later generations. Indeed, Gorgias himself had been famously disparaged and driven underground for much the same reason.

In other places at other times, the same pattern unfolds. For example, poets in eighteenth-century England, according to Anya Taylor (1979), became increasingly drawn to magic and witchcraft for an understanding of their own pleasure-centered linguistic craft, making much of the fact that writers, like magicians, seek to wield words and symbols in conjunction with "ecstatic possessed states of mind" (5). This occult approach to the question of authorial pleasure hoped to answer as well a "longing for the unpredictable, the distant, the vital, the turbulent" in an age that otherwise sought to reduce all knowledge to the conventions of rationality and science (3). Even in our own era, when people manifest this same impatience with generalized laws (in favor of immediate contexts), this same emphasis on transformative processes (rather than stable representations), and this same will-to-pleasure (as opposed to institutional, workaday rhetorical activity), they commonly draw upon magical or occult metaphors. For example, when Peter Elbow (1981) addresses the almost erotic pleasures of writing—the "inner juice" of words, the "gentle tug" that words can make us feel—he does so in a chapter of *Writing with Power* called "Writing and Magic" (357, 358).

Much like Gorgias, Ficino, and the others, Elbow has often been cast, if not scapegoated, as a figure at odds with the mainstream of his time. Specifically, many criticize Elbow as a figure too immersed in the "process"-revolution to comply fully with the "social turn" our field made toward matters of what David Bartholomae calls "academic discourse" and that occurred more or less concomitantly with the major phase of our professionalization. Elbow's thinking, from this perspective, is imbued with the ghetto-like working conditions that composition had so long endured. Indeed, to take an interest as Elbow does in magic/pleasure, according to William Covino (1994), is to take an interest in forms of knowledge and power that are explicitly remote from the centers of mainstream, "official" institutions. In short, magic and pleasure are not the stuff of insiders, not the stuff that David Bartholomae and the generation he so deeply influenced would associate with professional, academic discourse.

A Problem: Pleasure, Process, Professionalization

So divergent, in fact, are the aims of school-based rhetoric and the pleasure-oriented, magical tradition led by figures like Gorgias that Covino has characterized the latter as "renegade" (1988). This renegade line of thought values rhetoric not as "formulaic discourse" or pure technique, but rather as the activity of learning and wondering; a process that eschews the constraints of a singular "purpose or end or stance" and cultivates instead a "suppleness of mind" well-suited to address continuously evolving social contexts (44–45). This spirit of questing and ambiguity, this radicalization and tight braiding of process and context, Covino argues, can be found in Cicero, Montaigne, Vico, Hume, and others, all of whom met the mainstream rhetorical goals of unity, perspicuity, and closure—indeed, any information-based epistemology that would de-limit the associative play of the writer's generative forces—with distinct skepticism and resistance (1988, Chap. 2 and 3). This renegade strand is perhaps best exemplified in Thomas De Quincey's definition of rhetoric: to practice rhetoric is to "hang upon one's own thoughts as an object of conscious interest, to play with them, to watch them and pursue them through a maze of inversions, evolutions, and harlequin changes" (quoted in Covino 1988, 109).

But even the earliest renditions of "renegade rhetoric" are just as radical, if not more so. Gorgias, that first and most pleasure-centered rhetorician, left the fragment called *On Nature, or the Non-Existent* in which he says that there is no truth, and if there were, we couldn't know it, and, even if we could know it, we couldn't articulate it (1977, 128). This assertion implicitly but unequivocally champions the unbounded play of the verbal imagination. Thus, among the earliest utterances of what would become our field, we find an already renegade insistence on the free movement of language, an ecstatic, even orgiastic vision of words as the raw material of make-believe: "words," to revisit Gorgias' remark once, "are bearers of pleasure and banishers of pain" and we can come under their influence "as if ravished by the force of the mighty."

The constant refrain among all of these renegade rhetoricians is that the pleasure of rhetorical activity is thoroughly intertwined with a view of rhetorical activity as a process. The idea of process, of course, has figured importantly in the recent history of composition studies. The insight that composing-is-a-process marks a significant, even revolutionary moment in our field (Miller 1991, 121). For, having generated this insight, we could from that moment onward claim that we are not "merely" teachers, but active theorists and scholars who command and cultivate a significant body of knowledge. We could, for example, lay claim to a proud intellectual tradition of renegade rhetoric; we could create complex models of how the composing process works and what might hobble this process. Any number of intellectual tasks could follow, tasks that would give rise to new academic journals and fill books that would, in a generation, fill whole shelves. Thus, an eruption of magical, renegade rhetoric would appear to have been the star twinkling over the birth of contemporary composition as a profession.

But how could we presume to be, at once, both renegade and professional?

Indeed, when we reopened the ancient notion of selves, texts, and worlds as dynamic, interanimating processes, we underwent something akin to the therapeutic phenomena that interested Gorgias. That is, we enjoyed a thrilling reimmersion in the (academic) community after a century or more of displacement by literary scholars, and the stigma of our marginality showed signs of perhaps eventually dissolving altogether. Not surprisingly, this surging reversal of our long-standing alienation, this new sense of knowing and connecting, manifested itself as keen pleasure. Reflecting the mood of many of his colleagues, James Vopat described in 1978 the impact of Ken Macrorie's book, *Uptaught:* "the teaching of writing became a surprisingly exhilarating experience" (42). In this early phase of our professionalization, as process won ever wider support, students were encouraged to cultivate, through writing, their sense of the worth of their own experience and feelings. As Vopat puts it, "Their writing was engaging and often intensely personal," and he adds that as "the classroom gave up many of its deadening pre-70s Comp formalities . . . students, more quickly than might be expected, formed a circle of belief in each other and in their abilities." He concludes, "Students became expansive about the truths of their own lives" (42).

And yet, as Vopat argued more than twenty years ago, the "student-centered classroom places such a premium on personal truth that there is a resulting tendency to encourage and reward the sensational rush at the expense of the considered response" (42). And herein lies the paradox that perhaps divides our field at its very heart: the enthusiasm and pleasure, the "sensational rush," that colored our profession when it first began to form are, in a very real sense, unprofessional. That is, what spurred our rise in the institution and began to solidify us as a profession was a discursive force—something akin to what Robert Brooke (1987) calls "underlife"—that explicitly antagonizes both the "professional" and the "institutional" as we now understand them. Indeed, following what Covino delineates as the logic of institutional life that I noted earlier, we immediately articulated our fledgling insiderhood by banishing renegade themes (pleasure, process) back to the margins. We began to valorize "academic discourse," create doctoral programs, win tenure. And, of course, we reshaped our students' experience of our classrooms in fundamental ways. We simply cared a whole lot less about whether they experienced our teaching as "exhilarating" or their own writing as "expansive." Some of us, perhaps, cultivated a tough, surly skepticism about these possibilities as a primary source of authority and power.

Consider the most pleasure-centered rhetoric on the contemporary scene, *écriture feminine*, and its vexed relationship to the classroom. Its most celebrated advocate, Hélène Cixous, insists that this rhetoric "will never be able to be theorized, enclosed, coded . . ." (1986, 92). Most likely, the purpose of this sort of rhetorical activity—and its pleasure—is the transformation of phallogocentric reality, a process by which a Promethean femininity comes unbound and performs itself in the world. But even to suggest this much is to betray Cixous' insistence that *écriture feminine* will never be "theorized, enclosed, coded." Cixous' limited definition implicitly recalls Gorgias' remark about how there is no truth, and, even if there were, we could neither know it nor articulate it. And Cixous further echoes Gorgias' transgressive move against systematic thought when she chooses to signify this new extreme of renegade rhetoric with powerful blasts of imagery, a kind of poetic song or chant that overflows playfully with an excess of puns and sexually supercharged double-entendres. Here is what happens when one writes in the Cixousian mode:

> Unleashed and raging, she belongs to the race of waves. She arises, she approaches, she lifts up, she reaches, covers over, washes a shore, flows embracing the cliff's least undulation, already she is another, arising again, throwing the fringed vastness of her body up high, follows herself, and covers, uncovers, makes the stone body shine with the gentle undeserting ebbs, which return to the shoreless non-origin, as if she recalled herself to come again as never before. . . . She has never "held still"; explosion, diffusion, effervescence, abundance, she takes pleasure in being boundless, outside self, outside same, far from a "center," from any capital of her "dark continent," very far from the hearth to which man brings her so that she will tend his fire which always threatens to go out. . . . (Cixous and Clement 1986, 90–91)

Not surprisingly, important figures in our newly emergent profession have constructed this rhetoric as not simply renegade, but downright apocalyptic. As Lynn Worsham has eloquently argued, *écriture feminine* is not so much a theory of writing, but rather a "language 'event' that, in its more accessible moments, unleashes a damning critique and denunciation" of the norms of the academy (1991, 82). Because it explicitly opposes the ideals that necessarily govern our writing classroom (i.e., logical transitions, representational accuracy, stylistic clarity, and so on) any attempt we make to incorporate any element of *écriture feminine* into our pedagogy necessarily falsifies and de-fangs *écriture feminine*. According to Worsham's logic, a teacher who wishes to take this material seriously, to engage it honestly and on its own terms, must be prepared to "decimate . . . the university" (93). To do less is merely to colonize and trivialize this most ensorcelling discourse.

Worsham's point is well argued and, I suspect, fairly representative of the majority of those in composition who have wondered about the possibilities of this newest version of renegade rhetoric. What's most important to me, however, is the way it fits within the larger history of renegade rhetorics and their relation to the professional. Rarely, if ever, have we seen the renegade and the institutional set so far apart or conceptualized more clearly as locked in conflict. We see in Worsham's position on *écriture feminine* a repetition of Plato's on poetry. Like him, she would banish the experience of rhapsody as an essential threat to the social order on which her authority depends.

It seems to me, however, that any tidy division between *écriture feminine* and academic discourse is precisely the sort of thing Cixous, wave-like, would wash across. Her commitment to process and context presumably greets the conventions of the academy as so much *bricolage*, as convenient tools for the partial fulfillment of some particular purpose, tools to toss aside when one's purposes call for a different set of tools. In the Cixous passage I quoted, she describes the rhetor-as-wave not as destroying the cliff (an apt figure for the vertically organized monolith of the academy) but rather as embracing its "least undulation." She makes the "stone body shine with the gentle undeserting ebbs." In other words, renegade rhetorics offer us a shiny renewal, a transfusion of fresh vitality. As Cixous puts it in a slightly different context, "You only have to look at the Medusa straight on to see her. And she's not deadly. She's beautiful and she's laughing" (1990, 1239). Presumably, this laughter and all of the other pleasures of renegade rhetoric are redemptive rather than antagonistic in their relations with the academy.

Nonetheless, dominant traditions in our thinking have insistently constructed the renegade very differently—as antagonistic, combative, even apocalyptic. In this tradition, the body in general and pleasure in particular are the Medusa-like villains that pedagogy must vanquish, for they are not simply magical, but downright diabolical. For example, in the Middle Ages, as Walter Ong has noted, young men were sent to school to study Latin as a kind of puberty rite, an initiation or "hazing" ritual by which they were brought into the cult of the "gentleman," and this ritual involved not only the tedious memorization of rules, but also regular floggings (1971, 140). While corporal punishment for faulty declensions would seem passé, a distinct residue of this hazing ritual persists in our own era, for what else can explain the pattern of fury and ferocity that Joseph Williams notices in so much of our response to grammatical error (1981, 153)? While we rarely detect the errors that dot the texts of professionals, we actively seek them out in student texts and, when we find them, we figuratively slash them, often with "bloody" red ink. That is, we expose the texts as unclean, impure, and thus unfit for full membership in the academic community (see also Lees 1987). By embarrassing students this way, we slowly but surely initiate them into a certain set of affiliations, into a kind of membership that, as Patricia Bizzell (1986) and Richard Rodriguez (1993) both note, can unfold as a painful repudiation of their home culture. Indeed, the idea that pain is an essential ingredient in writing pedagogy would seem to explain why, whenever I introduce myself as an English professor, my interlocutor nearly always nervously retorts, "Well, I better watch my grammar!"[1] Clearly, we have not simply resisted the renegade, but demonized it, and, in so doing, we have not simply diminished the pleasures of awakening literacy but linked that experience, perhaps indelibly, to pain.

This pain may be a primary instrument by which the academy perpetuates itself. As Elaine Scarry claims, what is remembered in the body is remembered especially well: "It is not possible," she writes, "to . . . unlearn the riding of a bike" (1985, 110), for such knowledge, written in the skinned knees and bruised arms of the many awful tumbles off the thing, can never be erased. Scarry argues that pain dissolves the contents of a person's consciousness, clearing out this space to make room for the insignia of the regime that is inflicting the pain; and this is the mechanism by which institutions amplify their power, cell by cell, through a given population. While Scarry's topic here is the phenomenology of torture, surely a milder, more watered-down version provides the model for how, on a day-to-day basis, we proceed with the work of what David Bartholomae calls "inventing the university." When Bartholomae insists that he wants to create students "who know what I know and how I know what I know" (1985, 140), when he dismisses a concern for pleasure as the realm of "suckers" (1990, 128), when he insists that the chief objects of interest in our classrooms should be "power, tradition, and authority" (1995, 63), and, finally, when he and Anthony Petrosky open the introduction to their much-admired textbook, *Ways of Reading*, with the sentence, "Reading involves a fair measure of push and shove" (1993, 1), we must agree that we couldn't be much farther from the healing arts of Gorgias that launched what would eventually become our discipline, nor much closer to the flogging of would-be gentlemen that perpetuates "disciplinarity" as such.

I happen to like Bartholomae and Petrosky's textbook, *Ways of Reading*, very much, and the sorts of practical guidelines for teaching they set forth in *Facts, Artifacts, and Counterfacts* (1986) has perhaps influenced the day-to-day operation of my classroom more than any other single source. Their pedagogy, in constantly bringing texts into dialogue with each other and inviting student writing to take a seat at the table of these "cultural conversations," strikes me as supremely democratic and highly likely to inspire the sort of critical reflection in students that, to me, is a primary goal of academic discourse.[2]

But I find nothing short of alarming the ways this pedagogy can inspire a very real sort of totalitarianism. Working in the same tradition as Bartholomae and following the line of thought suggested by Bourdieu and Passerson in *Reproduction in Education, Society, and Culture*, Lynn Worsham conceptualizes the university in "Going Postal" (1998) as a black hole, a space of overwhelming gravity that traps and either annihilates or gives an unchanging shape to everything that drifts near it (see the epigraph to this chapter). Attempts to forge alternatives to this system are, according to Worsham, virtually certain to fail. That is, *écriture feminine*, like all other renegade rhetorics, is only a tool of the oppressor. Worsham writes, "To ensure its success, dominant pedagogy develops a system of subordinate educational ideologies that serve to mask its truth," and she continues, "philosophies and practices that claim to be non-violent and non-repressive are particularly useful in promoting misrecognition." She cites as examples,

> [P]edagogies (whether Socratic or psychoanalytic or ludic) that focus on the erotics of teaching and learning; or pedagogies (deconstructive or collaborative) that are premised on decentered authority in the classroom; or even pedagogies that emphasize affective understanding (feminist pedagogies of maternal nurturance) that exert power through the subtle instrument of coercion, the implied threat of the withdrawal of affection . . .

She concludes, "[T]hese projects serve to bind individuals and groups ever more closely to the authority of dominant pedagogy" (222). While Worsham maintains that "the struggle for social change must take place at the primary level of emotion" (223) and is obviously very much in favor of social change and a better understanding of emotion, she is, nonetheless, quite skeptical about the role pedagogy can play in this process, for she insists that "pedagogy provides and limits a vocabulary of emotion and, especially to those in subordinate positions, it teaches them an inability to adequately apprehend, name, and interpret their affective lives" (223).

Dominant pedagogy, in short, turns us to stone. The particular attempt to think about pedagogy in terms of pleasure, argues Worsham, simply repeats the "feel-goodism" and "sensitivity training" by which the contemporary workplace blunts the anger and bitterness that might otherwise force social change; this facile feel-goodism smacks too of the general waning-of-affect or birth-of-cool that Jameson associates with the oceanic commodification and consumerist sublime of advanced capital, and thus it panders directly to the pop-culture markets that we should instead challenge and resist (Worsham 1998, 229). Since pedagogy is inherently violent, Worsham implies, we must forego the temptation to dissemble in a haze of pseudo-enthusiasm for writing as a "touchy-feely" and "multi-culti" process of wonderment and growth.

Worsham offers persuasive evidence in support of her position. Specifically, she points to the fact that much workplace training, developed and authorized by industrial psychology, seeks to cultivate an emotional style in workers of empathy, friendliness, and consideration, a project that only drives anger "deeper into silence where it festers into rage" (225). She adds, "The result: workplace homicides have tripled in the last ten years" (225). Worsham's point is well taken, but I wonder if she may have too casually conflated the workplace and the classroom: while the feel-goodism she decries might indeed prove deeply irksome to workers who know they're being exploited, most students, I suspect, would be hard pressed to understand the ways their schools exploit them. Ignored, sure; betrayed, maybe; lied to, possibly. But it's difficult to see how a pedagogy of empathy, friendliness, and consideration could enrage students.

Student rage, I suspect, derives more directly from alienation, from a perception that pedagogy might *actually be* what Worsham says it is: a totalitarian machine designed to produce, coerce, even "clone" a certain legitimate kind of subject. In such a system, where student life-worlds are explicitly denied a place at the table of cultural conversations, is it any wonder that at least a tiny percentage of students will begin to dream of blowing up that table and everyone sitting at it? More precisely, doesn't such a pedagogy, by necessarily constructing gestures that point toward an alternative as apocalyptic, seem to invite precisely such a drastic response? If, as Mike Rose (1980) suggests, students will float to the mark we set and take on the identities we assign them, sometimes with a vengeance, then how can we be surprised when students become not simply disruptive, but downright murderous?

One thing seems certain: if the pleasures of writing have something to do with the practices of Gorgias and Cixous—that is, an experience of ongoing, open-ended connection with a community, a connection that runs counter to the abstract and otherwise marginalizing structures of entrenched institutional practice, something like what Robert Brooke calls "underlife"—then we might expect authorial pleasure, or something very much like it, to drive the formation of anti-institutional sub-cultures. Whether students become surfers, bikers, or hitchiking beatniks, whether followers of the diaspora of the Grateful Dead (Phish and other "jam bands") or simply transient "gutter punks," whether they become hackers who while away their lives in the endless slip-stream of the Internet or the slackers who mill around the wee-hour Ecstasy raves, each of these anti-institutional communities is undoubtedly a source of keen pleasure for its members, especially for those who feel otherwise marginalized or trapped. Certainly, the rowdy little Catholic youth group who set up the trailer behind the house where I was raised might fit this description. And we might understand violent street gangs like the Crips and the Bloods as partially analagous to these groups, and, too, the covens of young satanists who flirt darkly with blood rituals or the militia members who build bombs—each of these, and the Trenchcoat Mafia as well, might be understood as radicalized subcultures, groups who have heard too clearly the demonizing tones of dominant discourses and decided to play the role assigned them to the hilt.

I must, of course, stop far short of any gross oversimplification that would suggest that our field's "social turn" simply substituted a pedagogy of pain for the pleasure-based pedagogies of the process era and thereby helped lay the groundwork for the epidemic of school shootings. As Steven Schreiner recently argued, much process pedagogy implicitly valued a Modernist, belletristic tradition in which the most authentic writing is that which seeks to explore emotionally painful subject matter. Much the same point was made in the essay by Vopat that I've already had occasion to quote: he criticizes the process revolution for creating a model in which the best student writers are simply the ones most willing to poke their bruises. In short, even at the height of the process movement, an interest in pain overrode the full realization of what I've been identifying here as the renegade.

Perhaps the '70s interest in pain, however, sought to recontextualize it by talking about it inside the otherwise alienating confines of the university, a recontextualization akin to the therapeutic practices of Gorgias, one that sought to promote the classroom as a different kind of community, what Vopat called a "circle of belief" (1978) something like a subculture. Perhaps we can revise in important ways the '70s classroom that Vopat both praises and criticizes to make a different sort of dynamic between subculture and dominant culture, between renegade and institution, between the more radical aspects of the tradition we inherit and our obvious need to cultivate our status as disciplined professionals.

This point arises quite powerfully in Bruce Horner's recent work (2000) and in the work he has published with Min-Zhan Lu (1998). Adapting the ideas of bell hooks, Horner offers a devil's advocate sort of skepticism about our goal of establishing ourselves as professionals, a view that takes composition's nondisciplinary status "[N]ot as a lack to be corrected or a fate to be condemned, but as the basis for intellectual work that involves both students and teachers" (2000, 388). More specifically, this way of conceiving our marginality, as Horner notes in describing hooks' position, does not seek to "romanticize the oppressed or the experience of oppression, but to tap the potential for the marginalized to use that experience as a site of resistance, rather than defining it [exclusively] as a site of deprivation" (371). Horner is interested here—and more explicitly so in the essay he and Lu published together under the title "The Problematic of Experience"—in questions of academic knowledge production and the tensions between lore, phenomenology, and ethnography, whereas I am concerned with how the question of our marginality impacts our actual classroom practice.

More specifically, my questions are these: has the pressure that teachers of writing have felt in recent decades to "invent the university" amongst ourselves and in our classrooms and thereby to gain credibility on campuses across the country articulated itself as a certain refusal to empathize with students or to understand the worlds that created them? Still more pointedly, I must insistently return to the question Michael Blitz and Mark Hulbert ask in *Letters for the Living*: "As teachers of composition, are we ready for the truly powerful stories our students are ready to tell?"(1998, 1). Blitz and Hulbert underline the dire urgency of this question by borrowing from the 1996 collection *Schools, Violence, and Society*, which reports, among other heartbreaking facts, that the suicide rate among teens has quadrupled in the last three decades (Derkson and Strasburger 1996, 67).

A Solution and a Bigger Problem: Circles of Belief, Laughter, and Critique Versus the Masochism Machine

I hardly wish to suggest that we need only goad our students into writing like Cixous in order to assuage their alienation, anxiety, and rage. On the contrary, many of them, as late adolescents, are already suffused with distinctly renegade impulses, growing and changing at the fastest rate they will ever know in their lives; and the fact that they are undergoing this interval in the midst of the "postmodern condition," in which all of the metanarratives that have traditionally shaped and anchored both the self and the world are dissolving, means that they are already in a far more radical sort of Cixousian flight than any we could hope to offer, a flight that took off well before they've entered our classrooms and that likely will continue for a good while after they've left.[3] If anything, our students crave the reverse, the sort of structuring focus, commitment, and certitude that presumably they get—symbolically, at least—from their tattoos and piercings. I'll say more about this shortly.

Renegade rhetoric does not and cannot offer this sort of shelter, but it does offer a space for a particular sort of laughter, laughter that proceeds as a critical intervention against any structure that would prove more limiting than liberating. Again, this is not a move against the university, but a movement within the larger currents that are flowing through it. It implicitly asks us to accept the institution as more *porous* than we have heretofore, more available to the sorts of flights in which the pleasures of writing inhere.

Some of these possibilities have recently been developed at booklength in D. Diane Davis's *Breaking Up [At] Totality: A Rhetoric of Laughter* (2000). Davis describes a laughter that is intersubjective or transpersonal, and, in a phrase she borrows from Cixous, rooted in "the rhythm that *laughs you*" (22). This laughter runs counter to the naïve idealism that would cast academic discourse as a pristine vehicle for the realization of a rationalist utopia, and, more specifically, to the melancholic, Modernist hope that we can reconstitute any such reliable, foolproof foundation that, somewhere along the way, we lost. Despite its reversal of mainstream perspectives, however, this laughter is not combative, for it undermines the individuating structures of the subject who might presume to enact combat. That is, this laughter "respects no categorical distinctions and follows no social norms: it simply swoops in without warning . . . and challenges the ego by taking it for a spin through everything [and everyone] that was negated for the sake of its formation" (29). To elucidate yet further how this laughter works upon the ego, Davis draws an analogy to Zizek's account of some Romanian revolutionaries: "the rebels [are] waving the national flag with the red star, the national symbol, cut out," says Zizek, "so that instead of the symbol standing for the organizing principle of national life, there was nothing but a hole in the center" (quoted in Davis 2000, 46).

This tableau constitutes a powerful metaphor for the ways teachers who seek more pleasure-oriented pedagogy might come to see their mission. Instead of organizing ourselves around a central, transcendent ideal of "academic discourse" as that which names, masters, and controls reality, we need to sensitize ourselves and our students to the openings, cracks, and fissures in every discursive act, the holes in our flags through which the play, the laughter, and the general slippage of meaning flows. In this light, renegade rhetoric appears not as a purely alien force that threatens the academy from the outside as its binary opposite, but rather as an element always already inside its walls, but neglected and suppressed, sometimes even demonized, a force that not only can be let loose to play among us, but that slyly slides forth all the time of its own accord, most distinctly when we're enjoying the work that we do. Again, this mode of experience is not the opposite of critical thinking, for at the heart of both is that will to examine, delineate, and even celebrate the breaks, the cracks, the fissures and the holes in every text, exactly as the Romanian revolutionaries did when, before waving their flag, they cut a hole in it.

How might this work in actual practice? Consider a classroom activity that a colleague of mine, John Gery, uses to prepare his poetry students for particularly difficult reading. He first dissuades them from trying too hard to make sense of the text, from trying to make sense too quickly and too superficially. But before plunging into a discussion of what the particular text means, he asks students to write what he calls "unsense," random strings of words that observe no guiding principle other than the requirement that they have no intended meaning.[4] He then photocopies and distributes a few examples of his students' "unsense" and asks his students to interpret them, to make meaning out of them. Nearly always, he reports, his students come up with ingenious interpretations of these works that they know have no meaning until they themselves, as readers, construct it. This exercise has a playful quality, almost like a game, and it serves to relax the students and stimulate their creativity as readers. It places them in a much more productive relation to difficult, obscure writing. Perhaps most important, it liberates them not merely from the myth that meaning must derive from authorial intention but more broadly from the idea that "meaning" is purely a function of logic. That is, they see how texts come to have power and significance through what might be called their sonic properties: subtly structured rhythms or alliterative or assonant moments or syntactic parallelisms take hold of readers and prompt certain lines of interpretation. In short, the students come to see how large a share of meaning is really a function of the somatic pleasures usually associated with music. And thus, they acquire a genuinely material, technical capacity for critical thinking, a fine-grained sensitivity to nuances of style, that they can carry into any text they encounter. The students are thus invited into a subjectivity that links critical thinking to a sense of humor, of play, of spontaneous "creativity" and the power of sheer musicality, and this version of critical thinking strikes me as far more valuable than the vague pessimism or sour distrust that all too often passes in its place.

I've enjoyed considerable success with another exercise similar to the one I've just described. Again, it involves poetry. I first copy a poem onto the board (or the overhead projector, or the PowerPoint screen) and then have my students pick out its various formal features. We mark the strong and weak beats, the moments of significant enjambment or caesura that impact its tempo, and we code the rhyme scheme and any patterns of alliteration and assonance. I then erase the words of the poem itself, leaving in view only the notes about formal properties. I then ask the class as a group to fill in new words, words that conform, line by line, to the rhythmic patterns and poetic devices that we noted.

I stand at the board scribbling in their suggestions. I tell them not to worry about meaning at all, but just to mimic the sound, moment by moment, of the previous poem. What eventually emerges is, of course, almost wholly devoid of literal meaning. And yet my students find it impossible not to offer quite compelling interpretations, for the musical properties of the text they've created have them virtually spellbound. As one student put it, "I don't think we'll ever get to the bottom of our poem's meaning, but I bet it's the most meaningful thing any of us has ever written." My students, however, don't experience this excess of meaning as terribly heavy, binding, or authoritative. On the contrary, the process of creating the poem and playing with its possible meanings is always accompanied by wave upon wave of laughter.

Similar sorts of games can be played with passages of prose to yield much the same collective, renegade enjoyment. Importantly, this sort of pedagogic technique doesn't dispense with all rules and structures in an apocalyptic uprising, but rather uses structure (and even canonical literary texts) dynamically and for the deliberate cultivation of nonsense in order to sensitize students as critical thinkers in a material, hands-on way and to make their engagement with their own writing more rigorous, more pointed, and, ideally, more attuned to the power of *style*. They begin to awaken to the micropolitics of the four-way relations between author, audience, text, and world as these orbit around and suffuse every shift in rhythm, every turn of phrase. By this means, the pleasures of stylistic play form the basis for the rigors of ethical reflection.

Not only do these sorts of activities manage to generate both pleasure and discipline in student writers, but, in relying as they do on heavy doses of nonsense, they make the institution more porous. They constitute holes in what might otherwise seem an impenetrable monolith of authority and perfection; they create openings, spaces for laughter and play and the pleasures of musical language. These exercises constitute pathways of transgression, transgressions by which students who can't imagine having a warm engagement with their own imaginations, much less each others', move to an entirely new relation to the institution that has enabled that possibility.

Unfortunately, I fear that until quite recently our field has devoted precious little attention to these sorts of methods and goals. No matter how much poststructural theory we may have imbibed, we still succumb to the pressure to indoctrinate our students with academic discourse as something like the voice of mastery, a language that accurately "represents reality." Indeed, every composition program in the country probably includes in the boilerplate of its mission statement lines about requiring students to master the plain style and to produce "clear," error-free prose. When students seem less than inspired by this goal, we trot out notions of resistance which, as Richard Boyd and Marguerite Helmers have noted, have historically only essentialized students as flawed, deficient, and impaired by their refusal to follow the instructor's noble lead (Boyd 1999, 591; Helmers 1994, 10–11).

Therefore, I must begin to sum up and conclude this chapter by suggesting that, if Gorgias, Ficino, De Quincey, Elbow, Cixous, and the other renegade rhetoricians equate authorial pleasure with radicalized process-metaphors for both texts and selves and with rigorous immersion in particular communities, even personal contexts; and if we've often understood our institutional practice in a very different way, even pushing, at times, a totalitarian agenda in which we construct students and their works as static, stone-like objects that can be measured, evaluated, and discharged according to fixed criteria and mechanical, even codified notions of communication; then the writing that people do in school is very rarely pleasurable and, much more often, painful. Indeed, though I'll argue in the next chapter that a certain formality can be a rich source of pleasure, the particular way we've pitched writing instruction in recent years is such that, if students come to take any significant pleasure in any aspect of it, then that fact can only be attributed to our success in perverting them; that is, in making them masochists.

While it may seem utterly outlandish to define the experience of the typical writing student in terms of perversion, and while some may insist that my claims here border on the obscene, Gilles Deleuze insists that much masochistic fantasy would never set off the alarms of even the most vigilant censor. As Deleuze puts it, masochistic fantasy is so consumed with the tedium of mundane routines that it often imbibes the imagery of "national custom and folklore . . . or even the demands of morality and patriotism" (1991, 25). He might add that, with the rise of the massive disciplinary machinery that characterizes modern industrial capitalism, this perversion has become utterly pervasive, the signature of a new breed of human being. Today, we are all, in a sense, masochists. In this context, the purposes of pedagogy would be to produce precisely such a happily bound-and-gagged populace; the university, in this light, is essentially a machine for the production of masochism.

Much the same implication arises from an argument Mark Edmundson published a few years ago in *Harper's:* the '60s counter-cultural search for liberation and pleasure has devolved in our era into a quest for buying power and commodities, and our students therefore are ruled by a fear of losing the position that college would seem to afford them, a fear of falling off "the conveyor belt . . . onto the filth-strewn floor" (1997, 43). They rarely question anything or seek to crack open the uglier contradictions and inequities of advanced capitalism. They prefer, instead, to hold still, keep quiet and, stiff with consumerist "cool," they take their education as, at best, a kind of "lite entertainment." In other words, the project of education, according to J. Elspeth Stuckey (1991), is the enterprise of taking one's place in a particular regime or hierarchy; and getting an education, far from being any sort of liberation, is indeed the opposite, an experience of becoming "locked up" and learning to like it.[5]

When students write in the hopes of anchoring themselves in a particular niche, they do not write for the sheer adventure of the process. Rather, the only pleasure they know is the sort that comes when the writing is finished, when they can breathe a sigh of relief and feel "glad to have it over with." Instead of becoming absorbed in the process of generating new ideas and tinkering with them until a sense of connection with a particular audience arises, the students Edmundson and I have in mind have been taught to disavow this "renegade" terrain altogether and fetishize instead the final product. Indeed, these students feel that the process of working on the text unfolds as the necessary pain that enables the masochistic pleasure-as-relief to follow. They view the composing process as a kind of harrowing, dreadful, anxious experience of vertiginous flux, and the product that eventually emerges therefore must serve as a kind of bulwark, a safe haven or shelter against the dark fits and false starts of the process, as one small ticket in the larger set that entitles them to a particular array of comforts and securities.

So pronounced is this student distaste for writing that a good many of my colleagues in other disciplines jokingly report that whenever one of their course sections appears overenrolled, they need only assign a term paper to prompt a huge percentage of the students to drop the class. Our students cultivate this keen dislike of writing, because they have picked up innumerable indications from us that it is nearly impossible for them to win a place in the professional conversations of the academy. Even to begin to participate therein meaningfully or authentically, they must make an enormous sacrifice of energy, energy that they can only generate (in order to expend) by constructing a kind of dam or block in the ongoing stream of their mental lives, a kind of kink. They must strive to submit to a body of rules and conventions that they can only dimly perceive or understand, and they know that they are likely to fail and to provoke the censure of that body, an experience that will be embarrassing and painful.

By operating from the assumption that the composing process is devoid of pleasure and even painful, they compel themselves to build, more or less instantaneously, a reliable bulwark against it—a text so strong that it will never have to be reopened and revised. Even if the text turns out fairly shoddy, a great many of them will ardently resist revision and insistently construct revision as a kind of punishment. Students resist revision, according to Nancy Welch, because revision constitutes a kind of "deathwork"—that is, the act of dismantling and reconsidering an essay runs perilously close to the act of dismantling that fragile scaffolding of experiences, identifications, and beliefs we conjure and sustain as an ego (1997, 38).

Of course, a little deathwork, for most people, goes a long way. And the more one hates it, the more energetically one will seek to build a successful buttress against it. In our terms, the more one hates to write, the more one will seek to create a text that one will never have to rewrite, a text, that is, that even in its earliest conception is already emanating from a position that is bound-and-gagged in obsequious reverence for the overwhelming authority of "what-the-teacher-wants." In short, the most reliable road to an A+ is to cultivate acute displeasure in writing: the more it hurts, the better.

Deleuze argues that when someone engages that which they construct in advance as mundane, devoid of pleasure, or even painful, they can, by engaging it with sufficient rigor, slide into an experience of that which is "beyond the pleasure principle," the basis for all principles or laws, the sheer, unwavering, repetitive pulse by which difference or otherness endlessly reinvents itself, recirculates, and thrums rhythmically through language, consciousness, and our entire experience of being. In other words, that which is merely boring or stress-inducing can sometimes flower, in perversion, into a pumping whirlpool of pure otherness, of flowing erotic energy. Indeed, the struggle to censor the erotic, to control carefully the play of difference or otherness, to insist that some particular activity is mere humdrum, quotidian drudgery can cause its essential otherness to begin to repeat with particular heat. In the words of a fairly polite old proverb, "Push Nature away, and she'll return at a gallop." Yet more to the point, the cultivation of pain can become its own sort of pleasure. This is the project of masochism and the secret mission of dominant pedagogy.

When the masochist is "punished" for being "naughty," this purging of the erotic causes it to "return at a gallop." And the very activity of "punishment" then becomes saturated with ever-increasing erotic tension, the repetitive, wave-like slap of Difference. In a sense, the masochist is involved in a careful and studied journey into the heart of otherness or difference, and, as Deleuze argues in *Difference and Repetition*, into the heart of what psychoanalysis calls "the cure" (1994, 19). Through their suffering, masochists seek to come as close as they can to that raw particle storm of pure otherness or difference— what Lacan calls The Real, a space of purest anarchy that is intrinsically uninhabitable, a place in which pleasure and pain are mixed for the ultimate, agonizing apotheosis of pure Otherness, Death—so that they can capture it as completely as possible and thereby stave it off, perhaps forever.[6]

Students who visit the writing center I run regularly exhibit this kind of behavior. They come in, despondently holding a C- paper in their hand, and say, "I went over this paper over and over, like two dozen times, and I was sure I caught all the mistakes." They aren't quite sure, most of them, what mistakes might be there or even how to recognize them (much less how to fix them), but the torment of the repeated rereadings eventually comes to give them a twinge of pleasure that they take as an index to the effectiveness of their texts. They feel that both they themselves and their texts, having been immersed as thoroughly as possible via the rhythm of repeated rereading in the stream of pure Difference, are now happily harmonized, baptized, and aglow with an air of completion and peace. The tedium of going over and over the paper pushes "Nature" just far enough away to make the return a distinct experience, one they interpret as closure: "I feel pretty good about this thing and I guess that means I'm done."

Masochists are devoted to closure. They delight in having their hands tied, for freedom means an unmediated engagement with that raw particle storm of pure Otherness. Masochists do not simply ignore this harrowing, fiery throb but busily construct idealized objects to contain it or to buttress themselves against it. For Leopold Von Sachor-Masoch, the fetishized ideal is the dominatrix, and secondarily, her boots, whips, and furs. And Sachor-Masoch "constructed" her in a very literal sense: he taught her, coached her, cajoled her and persuaded her to deliver exactly the kind of experience he craves. For our students, the fetishized ideal at the center of their fantasy is the perfectly "correct," finished paper with an "A+" scrawled across the top, like the cherry on a sundae. For them, the boots, whips, and furs of Sachor-Masoch's mistress are replaced by the thesis sentence, the conclusion, and the effective, supporting details, all of which they have laboriously assembled just-so in the hopes that it will deliver the experience they crave: the sheltering web of entitlements, the niche or anchor, the "good-job-after-I-graduate."

This "good-job-after-I-graduate," which constitutes the sole lure that brings most students into the university, will in all likelihood be yet another version of the hot tedium of their schoolwork. Nonetheless, as a status symbol that defines for them a sense of identity and a sense of place, a distinct set of consumer options, they idealize it; and, in much the same way, they idealize the papers they write for us. That is, their papers are miniature versions of that same ticket into Being, that same buttress against Becoming.

In a sense, the student-masochists turn their idealized fetish-object into an embodiment of the Law, but they understand the Law in a particularly modern sense. While the Law was once conceived, before Kant and the rise of modernity, in terms of the Platonic Ideal of Goodness and the assumption that to obey the Law was to follow a program that is "best" for all concerned, the modern, masochistic subject intuitively understands, according to Deleuze, that the Law in the contemporary era has become severed from Platonic notions of Goodness and instead reinscribed as a wholly autonomous, arbitrary structure in itself, the object or purpose or basis of which can never be known. Masochists, argues Deleuze, therefore live their lives under this new conception of the Law and suffer daily the anxieties of a Kafka or a Prufrock: am I doing right and operating within the strictures of the Law or am I guilty and poised to suffer a terrible punishment? What should I be doing? How should I presume? Desperate for answers, this modern, masochistic subject seeks a feverish intimacy with The Law, an intimacy with that which is the source of all anxiety and which, as such, must be a secret reservoir of the pleasure that is otherwise withheld (1991, 88–89). That is, masochists enshrine the Law within their idealized fetish-object which thereby comes to symbolize—and buffer them against—the raw particle storm of pure Difference or Otherness. And then they bow down before it in deep gratitude, thrilled that it will allow itself to be known, thrilled that it will, in inflicting pain on them, clear their minds for the imposition of its own insignia, like a seal of approval, a stamped passport into a realm of yet greater security. Again, the greater the pain, the greater the success, and the surest road to good grades is to cultivate acute displeasure in writing, to disavow one's desire, pleasure, and power in homage to the nearest authority figure.

More specifically, this anxious will to construct an anchoring shelter, to bind themselves to the Modern, mysterious, post-Kantian Law in the hopes of being protected by it and from it, articulates itself in our classrooms nearly every time we distribute an assignment that is particularly open-ended or designed to promote significant reflection:

"Can you please tell us," the students beg us, "what you really want? What are we really supposed to do?" Their voices, in these moments, often keen with real yearning. One almost begins to feel that they are consumed with a mad meticulousness, as if they are suddenly such feverish perfectionists that their sole desire is to enslave themselves to the absolute letter of our criteria for success, as if they have sexualized what had heretofore been drudgery.

Students can, in fact, become so enslaved by the idea of the perfect, final textual product that their ability to actually generate readable prose is wholly undermined (see Rose 1980; Perl 1979). Deleuze would argue that "writer's block" is precisely the masochistic experience of being in chains, of being so trapped by an idealized vision of completion, that one can no longer roll along with the rhythmic thump by which Difference is forever recirculated and by which Being, in turn, embarks on infinite pathways of Becoming. When students cannot negotiate a way amidst and across the powerful flow of the composing process, they cannot generate prose. They submit a garbled wreck of an essay, get a D or an F, succumb to a yet more debased conception of themselves as wholly baffled and prostrated before the crushing authority of the academically successful; and, of course, they wind up hating school more than ever.

Miraculously, only a tiny percentage of them become ticking human time bombs. But I would wager that the vast majority of them know rhymes like those I shared at the outset of this book or, at the very least, would greet them with a dark snicker. Perhaps those who do start shooting are those who slip through the cracks of the masochism-machine onto the "filth-strewn floor," the particle storm of pure Difference or Otherness. The only security they can hope to win is that of the prison cell or the grave. I would hardly presume to point to my exercises with poetic language as an easy and certain antidote, but my students enjoyed them so much and seemed to benefit from them so much that I couldn't help but explore this way of teaching in more detail. I describe how I did it in the next chapter.

Notes

1. See also J. Elspeth Stuckey's *The Violence of Literacy* (1991); Page Dubois's *Torture and Truth* (1991).

2. I've borrowed the phrase "cultural conversations" from the title of a recent textbook by Stephen Dilks, Regina Hansen, and Matthew Parfitt (2001), one that offers a compelling extension of the sort of pedagogy associated with *Ways of Reading* by foregrounding the concept of history and the notion that discourses evolve over time. This particular focus, I find, gives students a useful

foothold in what can otherwise seem an all-too-authorititative body of discourse, one so powerful and entrenched that it strikes them dumb.

3. Those who have traditionally been "other-ized" (women, the poor, racial and sexual minorities) are surely experiencing a different version of this flight, one fretted with the turbulence generated by bitter, downwardly mobile white males who might struggle—often by violent means—to keep these Others in their place, to keep them from experiencing any such liberatory flight.

4. Despite Gery's helpful distinction here, I will soon revert to the more familiar word "nonsense" to denote language that has no intended meaning.

5. As Richard Miller (1996) writes, "The academy in general is not concerned with the production of writing that matters in the sense of providing a thera-peutic outlet for the author." Miller continues, "Writing that matters in the context of the academy is writing that establishes the author's position within the field of study" (278).

6. In the recent documentary, *Sick: The Life and Death of Bob Flanagan, Super-Masochist*, the subject of the film asserts that he is able to keep his terminal case of cystic fibrosis at bay, at least partially, by elaborate rituals of sexual masochism. Flanagan actually lived much longer than most CF sufferers, and he insisted with full confidence that his perversion enabled him to do so.

Two

Ancient and Contemporary Compositions That "Come Alive"
Clarity as Pleasure, Sound as Magic

I am driven to write, compelled by a constant longing to choreo-graph, to bring words together in patterns and configurations that move the spirit. As a writer, I seek that moment of ecstasy when I am dancing with words . . . toward the infinite.

—bell hooks, 2000

If clarity indicates a successful relationship between reader and writer, pleasure makes part of that success.

—Richard Lanham, 1974

The grim picture of student experience I've drawn in the last chapter is not, however, the whole story. As I noted, students do not *always* stagger hurriedly through the composing process in deep dread and anxiety. Sometimes, something enables students to bring real enthusi-asm to their assignments. Their intervals of inspiration, of pleasure, no matter what else we might profess to value, charm many of us and make us feel as though our teaching has at least partially succeeded. How we precipitate this pleasure in our students, however, resists formulation in a foolproof recipe, for just as these experiences are far too particularized, far too keenly rooted in immediate contexts to allow for an all-encompassing theory or general description, so too do they resist a fully guaranteed, rote method. Nonetheless, this chapter's epigraphs by bell hooks and Richard Lanham offer important clues to the theoretical question of how, in general, pleasure can blossom in the act of writing, as well as to the more practical question of how we can, without reducing our students to mere masochists, help them enjoy the work of producing clear, even powerful prose.

"Clarity," of course, is a well-worn, but rather misleading metaphor: language is never a transparent window into some extra-linguistic reality. Rather, clarity, as Lanham suggests, really refers to an experience of connection between author and audience, an experience of the transpersonal dimension of language, something like the experience, as bell hooks notes, of becoming swept up in dance. In fact, when hooks compares writing to choreography, she reminds me of that important breakthrough in my teaching I discussed in the previous chapter, those classroom exercises with poetic language.

I hardly intend to advocate any sort of empty, lockstep formalism, in which students march through fill-in-the-blanks drillwork, nor do I push my students to produce language unduly weighted with stylistic ornaments. Rather, I've simply decided to introduce my students to a set of stylistic devices and principles as a kind of interim measure toward getting them to listen to language more carefully. I hope that, as my students develop an increasingly "objective" relation to language, perhaps they will eventually learn to make words dance and dance well enough ultimately to approach that circle of belief in which reader and writer, self and other, are drawn so tightly together that it feels as if the thoughts of one person are becoming the thoughts of the other, an experience in which any delimiting boundary between reader and writer seems, at least for a fleeting instant, altogether impossible. This experience is the opposite of the masochism I delineated in the last chapter—not a locking down and staving off of the Otherness-within that sparks change and growth, but its cultivation. This, I think, is what bell hooks calls an experience of "the infinite."

Some might suggest that I'm being awfully grandiose, given that what I'm calling "the infinite," we have traditionally referred to as mere "clarity." But I like hooks' term. It underlines and lays bare the very real profundity of the phenomenon we want students to be able to precipitate and, too, it helps me to think about what Richard Lanham points to as its principal feature: that is, pleasure. I should hasten to add that what I'm proposing is hardly any sort of holy grail that will end once and for all the search for a perfect pedagogy, one that students will instantly love and that will permanently assuage the age-old concerns of teachers and administrators. Instead, what I offer here will, I hope, help us move beyond, in a partial and limited way, the impasse in which our impulses to inspire students and help them enjoy writing would seem to run counter to the goal of acquainting them with the conventions that enable them to write effective prose.

More particularly, I've chosen to explore a way to teach renegade rhetoric—that highly pleasurable practice in which selves, texts, and worlds are experienced as dynamic, interanimating processes—in a way that honors the need for certain structuring, teachable, concrete strategies.

Neither Voice Nor Discourse:
Sophistry and the Power of Sound

I'd like to begin, however, by specifying what a pedagogy that would aim in this direction is *not*. First, I am not simply advocating a so-called free or open classroom, nor a pedagogy that emphasizes revision as a potentially endless or infinite process. In that sort of utopian classroom, particular drafts become unimportant, or, at least, have no more social footing than random watercolor doodles done by blindfolded students, for, no matter what a student writes in such a context, it can always be rewritten again and again. While I remain very much interested in reviving the notion that writing is a process I want to link, rather than oppose, this idea to the obvious fact that writing is also a product. I think we have limited our understanding of how to teach the writing process by defining it, as we have ever since Donald Murray's 1972 manifesto "Teach Writing as a Process, Not a Product," as the opposite of studying literary models and learning to appropriate their formal devices. Instead, I would like to define in this chapter a pedagogy that collapses this binary, one that advocates multiple drafts, and, at the same time, considers the ways the formal features of finished products—stylistic figures, schemes, tropes—can actually play a powerful role in the drafting and revising process. These stylistic devices can help the student string together sequences of moments in their texts, help them choreograph these moments toward an increasingly grand moment of powerful connection between reader and writer.

Another qualification: this pedagogy by no means seeks to distinguish the domain of feeling from that of thinking, learning, and knowing, for, as recent generations of feminists have taught us, such binaries are logically untenable and usually only serve to mask highly assymetrical gender relations (i.e., masculinity equals rationality or The Good; femininity equals mere feeling or The Bad). Instead, this pedagogy explicitly operates from a middle ground where the two domains of thinking and feeling are indistinguishable. Similarly, this pedagogy does not seek to goad students into a purely histrionic, confessional mode, for, as valuable as such personal writing can be, it doesn't necessarily, by itself, acquaint students with the sorts of rhetorical tools they need for generating power in the world. Moreover, the connection between reader and writer that I want students to learn how to build is not to be confused with the sort of passion that Jane Gallop describes (1997) and that may have made her vulnerable to charges of sexual harassment. While strong emotions and personal experiences can play a key role in good writing, the focus of the writing classroom I'll describe here is always on writing itself— that is, on writing, in a highly technical sense, *as writing*.

Moreover, this pedagogy does not foreground emotion itself as an isolated object of inquiry. Despite the considerable value, for example, of historical research into the ways that different rules for the experience of pleasure have been enforced by different power structures and applied in varying ways to subjects with different race and class affiliations and different sexual identities, this inquiry into what Raymond Williams calls historical structures of feeling (1977, 128–31) offers no particular pedagogic method that applies directly to the specific challenges faced by writing teachers. Similarly, this pedagogy does not provide instruction in what Megan Boler describes as "emotional literacy" (1999), in which students are taught to be more sensitive to each other, to resolve conflict, to subdue their emotions, and to develop a more expansive and nuanced vocabulary to describe emotion. On the contrary, my classroom seeks not simply to enable students to "express" their emotions or "resolve" their conflicts, but rather to refine, communicate, and negotiate their differences more pointedly by uniting the cultivation of inward feeling as a moral register with an immersion in certain technical aspects of prose. In other words, the emotion this classroom would seek to cultivate, over all the others, is the pleasure of connection between reader and writer, a connection that doesn't exclude but rather rests upon a rich capacity for debate and a rigorously practical sort of critical reflection about language.

What I propose is a pedagogy that differs significantly from the transcendentalism of the expressivist approach to writing pedagogy and its highly individualistic pleasures of "voice" that, through the late 1980s, were heavily attacked and largely discredited. Of course, many might assume that any pedagogy interested in pleasure is necessarily expressivist, so I'd like to linger a moment over the differences between the goals attributed to expressivism and what I'm advocating here. Expressivists allegedly believe that no one can really teach anyone else how to write, for good writing originates in the innermost depths of the private individual; instead, the expressivist strives to create a classroom atmosphere in which the student is free to access his or her own, individual "true voice." Expressivism's underlying metaphor, as Peter Elbow puts it, "is that we all have a chest cavity unique in size and shape so that each of us naturally resonates to one pitch alone" (*Writing with Power*, 1981, 281–82). What expressivists value most is this sense of voice, for it distinguishes a piece of writing as coming from a particular author, and, as such, is closely related to the idea of *ethos* or personae. At the same time, as Joseph Harris suggests, voice in the expressivist view is also, importantly, a kind of prized quality, for the more a writer has a sense of her own voice, the more "voice" she'll get into her text, and the more successful that text will be, for voice is what gives the text what Elbow calls "juice" and "electricity," and makes it more and more "real." This way of thinking about voice is tied with our field's interest in the growth of the "whole person" (1997, 25), for the more we can help students find their voices, in this sense, the more we enable them to use language as a tool for authentic self-discovery and self-expression, to access a self that transcends the deadening constraints of school and the wider culture, even the constraints that accompany the goal of communicating with others.

Many have condemned pedagogies that emphasize the expressivist version of voice, for, as Harris points out, expressivists are more interested in rendering experience than analyzing it, and, as such, they tend to sidestep the broad intellectual project of developing shared understandings. Instead, the detractors of expressivism favor a way of thinking about voice that at first seems rather awkward or counterintuitive, and that, as I'll argue here, is just as limited, though in a different way, as the one attributed to expressivism.

For expressivism's critics, voice should be understood as discourse. "Instead of starting with the idea of a personal voice that comes from within, from a 'chest cavity unique in size and shape,'" argues Harris, "we need to begin with the idea that our culture speaks to us through many competing voices" (34). Harris offers as examples of what he is talking about the voices of home, school, neighborhood, work, leisure, childhood, parenting, youth, age, friendship "as well as the various fields and methods that make up our ways of knowing" (34). He adds, "a voice [is] a way of speaking that lies *outside* a writer, and which she must struggle to appropriate or control." Harris explains that not only is voice *not* an extension of the self, but that the self, too, is *not* some sort of mysterious, primordial essence that transcends the social sphere and gives rise to voice as a spirit-like quality that makes writing more "real." Rather, those who criticize this expressivist notion argue that the self exists only as a set of perspectives on or relationships with other entities. Thus, many of them advocate the sort of pedagogy associated with David Bartholomae and Antony Petrosky, in which the student doesn't seek to escape conventions or liberate a transcendent self and its "true" voice, but rather to try on the particular, conventional voices/discourses of the university and use them as tools to reconsider, in turn, the stock notions of common sense, the naïve routines, stereotypes, and all-too-"clear" discourses that govern our experience of the everyday world. Harris suggests that this way of thinking about voice (as discourse) allows for far more rigorous teaching and learning; where the expressivist classroom favored an uncritical rendering of experience, this one urges us to explore our experiences critically, testing the discourses we might use to describe them and the nature of the events themselves in a general project of acquiring more skeptical and sophisticated habits of thinking.

This more complex understanding of voice (as discourse) has surely made a great many of us far more effective teachers than we could hope to be in the earlier, more naïve paradigm. But I fear that this view, representative as it is of the now dominant view in composition theory, has left certain loose ends dangling and obscured certain useful dimensions of the expressivist version. More specifically, while I very much like the practice of having students read an assemblage of essays on some particular theme (home, work, friendship, and so on) and then sort out a position vis-à-vis the tensions or gaps among the readings, a position that says something more or less original about the readings and about the students' own lives, I worry that to discuss voices/discourses in such general terms obscures crucial details in the ways we encounter and learn to use them. Though a thoroughly appropriate theoretical description of the goals of our teaching, it explains very little about what actually happens at the level of lived experience and daily practice as students develop the abilities we want them to have. In short, I find nothing in this theory that accounts for how we encounter these voices in a direct, material way as different *styles*; in simplest terms, it neglects an experience that is vital to the developing writer, the experience of how a particular piece of writing sounds.

When Harris writes about the voices of home, of work, of friendship, and so on, I can't help but wonder what they sound like, how they compete for the trust that sooner or later I have to give to some of them over others, what role the winning of this trust plays in the larger project of persuasion, and how I can best attune my students to the sound of this all-important credibility to help them gain a share of it. In other words, I've never been certain of what exactly Harris means by voice: for him, disciplinary methods are a kind of voice, and so is the voice of "the neighborhood." I understand the connection, of course, but only in a highly generalized, abstract way, and I worry that, in this significant departure from the stream of spontaneous, sensory experience, certain powerful tools for teaching, learning, and writing are being left behind.

And so, I decided to revive aspects of the earlier concept of voice, but to deliver them from the naïve expressivist school as well as from the overly abstract concept of mere "discourse." That is, I decided to explore ways to teach students about voice in terms of how their writing sounds. While the domain of sound might seem awfully nebulous, I've taught this powerful dimension of our experience of writing very concretely through a practical, even quasi-formulaic interest in prose style, and I've tried to push questions of prose style constantly toward questions of ethics.

That earlier, expressivist model of voice obliquely touches on the power of sound as I intend to delineate it here. Unfortunately, as Harris and many others would surely point out, that version of voice usually miscasts the power of sound as the driving force in an apotheosis of purely individualistic personality. More specifically, when Elbow speaks of how each of us "resonates to one pitch alone," I think he's quite right to talk about a deep sense of how we want our texts, quite literally, to sound, but the idea that each person has his or her own particular pitch wholly reverses the important truth that Elbow's comment is on the verge of articulating. That is, when he talks about writing that has "juice" and "electricity," writing that we experience as "real" or "meaningful," he is not pointing, as so many claim he is, to an apotheosis of individual personality, but of the opposite: an apotheosis of the transpersonal. The writer, in such passages, connects with readers because he or she has tapped into that which exceeds the author as an individuated source of meaning. In short, the writer has tapped into the power of sound. When writers access the profoundly social force that is sound, they create as well a vital opportunity for critical reflection: in simplest terms, stylistic choices are also ethical choices.

Much this same implication arises in Elbow's award-winning but too-seldom-cited essay from the mid-1980s, "The Shifting Relationships Between Speech and Writing" (1985, 1999). What he says about speech opens the way for how I've come to think about sound as a broad category that involves timing and tone (or ethos, and, in turn, ethics) and, most concretely, stylistic devices and principles. Instead of addressing the rhetorical value of sheer personality, Elbow traces in this essay certain "speech-like" qualities that we would do well to cultivate in our students' composing processes: speech is spontaneous, prompted by immediate contexts, usually as an explicit reply to something else that has been said, and it proceeds with a distinct rhythm, asking the listener to engage the words closely, filling in and following implications as needed, participating in the dance of the speaker's mental events. Elbow adds that the best teachers know how to prompt their students to capitalize on the oral language skills they already possess (179). That is, good teachers know that when they're working with a student whose prose is so badly scrambled as to be more or less impenetrable, they need only "ask the student to *say* what she was getting at," and then the student will almost always articulate her point in ways that are "perfectly clear and lively" (180). The clearer, spoken version need only be transcribed, and the paper is then well on its way to considerable improvement.

This talk-based technique works quite well in many of the tutoring sessions in the writing center that I run, for it exploits a skill all native speakers have acquired long before they've reached college, a skill for managing language *not* as an objective entity resting statically in space (of the sort Harris implies when he lists the monolithic "voices of . . . work and leisure, childhood and parenting" and so on) but as a dynamic event that unfolds in and through time. As Elbow notes, we can take in only a few words at a time, never a whole document at once, and therefore the rhetorical skills of style and arrangement involve leading the reader/listener on a journey through time, using language to record a parade of "live mental events" in such a way that they'll live again, parade again, in the minds of readers.

The transformative powers of time are inherent in speech, for speech, as Elbow notes, is spontaneous, rhythmic, and rooted in the immediate, ongoing context of dialogue. Although these seem like relatively ordinary features of the temporal quality of speech, they come to inhabit our writing only during "magical" intervals of inspiration, which are, for most of us, all too rare. More specifically, when our writing proceeds fluently rather than in tortured fits and starts, with rhythmic thrust rather than in diffuse, undisciplined clumps, and with the feeling of a reply to an interlocutor who is immediately present rather than with a hazy sense of there being little possibility of ever actually being read, when all of these conditions apply, we are inhabiting a mysterious, highly pleasurable territory that all successful writers have learned to cultivate and, when they sit down to write, to summon with some fair degree of consistency.

By deliberately imagining this experience of dialogue as we compose and thus stylizing our sentences with distinctly rhythmic figures of various kinds, we can begin to lay claim to a sort of temporal power, a momentum, something like the sheer spontaneity of thought, that our readers can perceive and experience as well. In fact, this curious power and pleasure, this "inspiration" is purely an affair of carefully stylized language. This point was made quite succinctly by one of my students, Tharon McDowell, who, a few weeks after I introduced the class to stylistic figures of various kinds, said, "These stylistic devices help me incorporate the way I talk into my writing." And another, Brad Monnet, said, "These devices make an ordinary, dry sentence come alive," which, he added, "keeps the reader more interested." When my students say that their writing is better when it incorporates aspects of their speech, I don't think they are simply suggesting that their writing is better when it slips into the vernacular and drifts away from academic rigor. I think, instead, that they're referring ultimately to their experience of sound, for sound has a unique power to override the individual will, to promote experiences of connection between people, to keep "the reader more interested."

I can best explain what I mean by contrasting the experience of hearing to that of eyesight, for eyesight far more thoroughly undergirds the will than does hearing, and it therefore lends itself more readily to the phenomena of individuation. For example, I can turn to look to the left or I can turn to look to the right or I can choose to close my eyes to stop looking altogether. Sounds, on the other hand, override my will, for if a jet passes overhead right now, I will hear it whether I choose to or not—but I will only see it if I deliberately get up, go to the window, and search the sky. This binary, of course, is by no means absolute: musicians will surely tell us that hearing can involve an enormous intensity of the will, and visual artists, conversely, will likely describe all sorts of experiences of surrendering to the pleasures afforded by their eyes. Nonetheless, sounds, much more than sights, have a dynamic, event-like power, a power to undermine the structures that individuate the subject, a power that is manifest much more rarely in visual material. To put it in simplest terms, we can willfully close our eyes anytime we wish, but we can never really close our ears. Sounds capture our attention; they have the power, moment to moment, to change us. Sound, in this sense, is something like a distillation of time itself. This, I think, is what my students are talking about when they say they are bringing their writing closer to speech through the use of stylistic devices: not the dubious rhetorical value of sheer personality or "true voice," but the opposite, the transpersonal, transformative force of sound.

To attune my students to this force, I decided to teach them to attend closely to the process of generating sentences, something most teachers of writing no longer do. Though our field had, in the late 1970s, a richly developed rhetoric and pedagogy of the sentence—the generative sentence-rhetoric of Christensen, imitation exercises, and, of course, sentence combining—our field increasingly moved away from this approach in the early 1980s. As Robert Connors argues, these pedagogic techniques seemed to improve student writing, and no research ever proved otherwise; what's more, students seemed to show great enthusiasm for them. The only problem with them, as Connors argues, was in the way this material was presented—that is, in the exercises themselves (2000, 115). Connors quotes James Moffett, who says, "For the learner, basics are not the small-focus technical things but broad things like meaning and motivation, purpose and point, which are precisely what are missing from exercises" (110). What Connors doesn't mention, however, strikes me as precisely what's most curious about the exercise-oriented version of sentence-level pedagogy: that is, sentence-level pedagogy reached its zenith of popularity in the late '70s and early '80s, the moment that was also nearly the height of the process movement.

Why can't we link the two great passions of that era and thereby revive them? Why reduce an interest in style to mere exercises when these devices have such generative power, can so readily focus revision, and thus so easily play a role in process-based pedagogy? Why *not* teach these stylistic devices explicitly as tools for invention and revision, as a means to create and craft sentences and paragraphs, to choreograph writing so that it can participate in the flight of time the way speech does, so that it can resonate with that same fullness of spontaneity, contextual immediacy, and distinct rhythms? Indeed, when writing is most successful, it passes through time, as bell hooks says, to yield an experience of the infinite, the dimension in which the boundaries that delimit and differentiate writer and reader, self and other dissolve. After all, to write so engagingly, as Lanham (1974) puts it, is simply to write "clearly."

Therefore, rather than focus students on style through a series of exercises, my pedagogy explicitly presents the work of practicing these techniques as a form of play. I try to emphasize play not simply as something children do, but also as something that musicians, actors, and athletes do, something they do with utmost discipline. Though each of these people might seem to "play" very differently, for all three of them playing implies a performance that unfolds *in and with time*. In fact, a spirit of play, argues John Dewey, characterizes the best classrooms—not simply as an expedient, temporary reprieve from the tedium of real schoolwork, not just as an aimless amusement for the immature, but rather as a process of serious absorption in an activity that, in its purest form, takes as its primary goal only the endless continuation of the activity itself. In other words, while play might yield tangible results, these are not really the purpose of the activity but something more like incidental souvenirs or toys that serve only to spur yet further, more pleasurable continuation of the activity, openings by which the activity accesses an ever greater experience of eternity or the infinite.

The best teachers, Dewey suggests, ultimately want the attitude of play to permeate the students' concept of work, for "Work which remains permeated with the play attitude is art" (1994, 194–206); and art, for Dewey, is that which constantly nourishes and renews the imagination, and, in turn, the entire culture. As a writing teacher, then, my goal has become not simply to avoid turning students into masochists, but to turn them into artists by teaching them how to play with prose style.

These stylistic principles and devices, while often described as the tools that oralist rhetors of old might have used to make their texts more easy to memorize, can also be used to generate a dynamic experience of time or timing that is highly pleasurable, even "magical" for both reader and writer. Again, this particular interest in timing is as old as rhetoric itself, for, as James Kinneavy and Charles Bazerman both note, the ancient concept of *kairos* imbued nearly all early thinking about rhetoric. This concept translates roughly as a sense of temporal appropriateness, of the opportune or fortuitous moment, a sense not simply of saying the right thing but specifically the right thing *at the right time*. Although *kairos* is most often used to refer to rhetorical situations as located in time, the concept clearly has implications for making local decisions within a particular text, how to sequence, arrange, and *time* the specific effects one seeks to achieve, to make them, as my students put it, do what speech does: that is, "come alive."

To clarify how and why I've begun to foreground matters of style in my writing classes, I want to begin by linking it to what is perhaps the oldest method for teaching composition, the very first insight of the Sophists, the one from which their writing pedagogy sprang. As Jacqueline De Romilly tells it in the opening chapter of *The Great Sophists of Periclean Athens*, the sophists were "a handful of men active for the span of roughly one generation" (1992, 2) who appeared in Athens in the middle of the fifth century with a bold promise. They would provide to anyone with the means to pay for it an education that would enable that student to play a distinguished part in the life of the city (4). They were, in a sense, composition's first professionals, but the understanding of writing-as-a-process that interested them was not stuck in binary opposition to the experience of literary models, but instead was explicitly based, as I'll show, on the temporal or kairotic experience of the poetry of the rhapsodes. As such, the sophists offer a powerful resource for the contemporary discipline of composition as it struggles to define itself as a profession without losing the renegade powers that have always been its heart and soul. What I'm suggesting, on one hand, is hardly new: in fact, figures as diverse as Susan Jarratt, Jasper Neel, and Victor Vitanza, all prominent voices in our discipline, have identified themselves one way or another with the sophists. A full generation ago, Edward P. J. Corbett and Richard Lanham made much the same move I'm making here when they published lists of rhetorical terms, tropes, and stylistic devices, all of which they borrowed directly from the sophistic tradition. More recently, Arthur Quinn published *Figures of Speech: Sixty Ways to Turn a Phrase*, Sharon Crowley and Debra Hawhee wrote a textbook called *Ancient Rhetoric for Contemporary Students*, and Robert Harris published *Writing with Clarity and Style*, each of which features page after page of sheer verbal technique.

These formal devices are the very things the sophists sold to their students: techniques for speaking in public, for defending and advancing one's interests in courts or civic assemblies (De Romilly 1992, 6), for organizing language dynamically as a sequence of moments that, if choreographed well, will open that powerful, transpersonal force of clarity that, at its strongest, has been associated with inspiration, magic, and the infinite.

The sophists quickly extended their interest in verbal techniques to political philosophy and from there to modes of human behavior. Eventually, they began to "note down and classify a whole mass of data relating to all areas of life" (8), so much so that, for example, when one of them, Thrasymachus, was passing away, he composed for his tomb an epitaph that ran "Chalcedon was my country, knowledge my profession" (1). Sophists, De Romilly explains, explicitly distinguished themselves from sages and philosophers, for these terms imply, respectively, a state of being and the patient, distinterested search for truth, whereas the sophists cast aside both in favor of cultivating the magic-like power to manipulate social reality and achieve certain effects in their immediate surroundings (1). For the sophist, De Romilly points out, knowledge "was their specialty, just as the piano is the pianist's" (1).

The analogy of sophistic knowledge to musical knowledge couldn't be more appropriate, for, as Stephen Katz (1996) argues, at the core of the sophistic practice of knowing was a preoccupation with the sound of language. More specifically, the sophists led a sweeping dismissal of the gods and a powerful critique of all forms of transcendental philosophy, following instead the assertion of Protagoras that "Man is the measure of all things;" but they went even further to doubt the power of the human senses to discern reality and truth. Given the absence of any reliable cognitive anchors—no gods, no transcendent ideals, not even any reliable sensory faculties—what leads men and women to construct and live in their world one way rather than another, according to the sophists, is the sheer magic of the *sound* of how they speak to each other. The pleasures of verbal style, as Katz writes, were seen as far more than just "irrational sensations;" they were "fundamental to knowing" (89). The sophists, says Katz, felt that knowledge could not be developed by rational inquiry but rather "was created in and (through response to) poetic arrangement and style" (88). The power of language, he adds, is rooted in the "musical property of words," and this power always takes a sensuous form that creates feeling, thought, and reality by evoking sensory action. For this reason, rhetoric as the study of style is the primary focus of education, culture, and even humanity. It is the root of all knowledge (93).

My students intuitively seem to understand this idea without having it explained to them, and, too, many of them find this "musical property" to be a sharp spur to critical thought. For example, toward the end of a class period early one semester, I asked my students to freewrite for a few minutes about what they took to be the most important ideas to have emerged during class discussion. Then, after I stopped them, I told them to look back through what they had written and craft some particular moment of it into a syncresis—that is, a comparison-contrast that proceeds in parallel clauses, such as "Cowards die a thousand deaths—heroes die but once." Within a few moments, several of them were ready to share their attempts. Some, as it turned out, were perfect, and others needed to be tweaked slightly to fit the form. After hearing a few of them, a particularly earnest student, Charlie O'Connor, raised his hand rather tentatively with a perplexed look on his face. "You know," he began, "I'm not so sure about this. When I hear these sentences, they really sound good—they've got that feeling, that literary feeling, so I just know they gotta be true." I replied, "But there's a problem, isn't there?" And Charlie quickly shot back, "Well, yeah. Anytime anything sounds that good, I get suspicious and can't help but question it. With some of these sentences, I agree, but others I'm really not sure about."

I told Charlie how pleased I was to see him engaging in this kind of critical reflection and that I hoped he would keep cultivating that capacity all semester. Our purpose, I said, was not simply to surrender to the pleasures of that "literary feeling" but to develop an increasingly refined sense of what that "literary feeling" might have the power to conceal. And I added that a moving piece of language, when we're learning how to write, should move us at least partly to question where that moving feeling comes from and how it works. And, as easy as it is to let these sorts of figures pass without thinking critically about them when they appear in isolation, they prove even more slippery when many of them are embedded together in a larger swatch of prose.

In fact, when a good many sentences are stylized rhythmically, they can really carry us off our feet or at least lull us into nodding agreement. After all, that's what they were originally designed to do. These rhythmic techniques, as Eric Havelock explains, originally served the rhapsodes in ancient Greece, in the era before the advent of writing and the rise of the sophists, as tools for memorizing the vast cultural encyclopedia that they were required to recite, and through which they exercised enormous power (1963, 145). These techniques allowed the rhapsode to weave and reweave the vast repository of cultural memory into a heavily stylized, easily remembered tapestry; in short, they enabled the past to "come alive" and persist into the future, and this highly pleasurable re-creation engendered something like what Emile Durkheim calls the *mana*-feeling, a communal feeling of collective self-knowledge (O'Keefe 1982, 166).

This feeling, according to Daniel O'Keefe, first occurs during dramatic group activities, a feeling that the group then symbolizes with *mana*-objects which gradually come to constitute the sacred sphere; around these objects, certain beliefs and rites take root, which, once organized, become religion (187). Once a religion becomes formalized, fragments of the *mana*-system can be broken off, isolated, and reorganized to antagonize or at least dialogue with the larger *mana*-system, and this activity, according to O'Keefe, is what we traditionally identify as the practice of magic. Examples might include the Black Mass, voodoo, tarot cards, the Ouija board, and so on.

This process by which religion is created and then fragmented to give rise to magic explains, too, how the rhapsodes made possible the careers of the sophists. The fragments that the sophists appropriated from the rhapsodes were, of course, the stylistic devices. These units of musical technique in language could be used to dialogue with the collective and precipitate such extraordinary experiences of pleasure as to seem magical. The stylistic devices still seem to have a magical quality, for they strike students as part of an ancient, esoteric knowledge system, one that can provide them with considerable power. In fact, when I first introduced my students to concepts like syncresis and zeugma and so on, they nearly unanimously responded with comments like, "I've always heard and read sentences that were set up this way, but I had no idea there were names for these patterns, much less that anyone could actually plan to use them."

When my students asked me how and why these techniques manage to stir such strong feeling, I suggested that all of them are essentially ways of creating and manipulating the experience of rhythm. I draw on Havelock's work to say that by encoding certain repetitive patterns into our discourse, we allow for a wide variety of oral utterances that repeat the same structure of movement between the lungs, throat, tongue, and teeth, and, even when we're silently reading, our vocal cords register regular patterns of movement (Katz 1996, 137). Perhaps we feel these rhythms spreading, sending scarcely perceptible signals to related parts of the body as an essential element in processing abstract chains of symbols. These patterns of repetition might organize various complex motor reflexes to such a degree that they operate without any need on the part of the subject to think about them; that is, the act of communicating proceeds in ways roughly analogous to "similar reflexes of the sexual or digestive apparatus" which are "highly sensual and closely linked with physical pleasures" (Havelock 1963, 149). For example, mechanisms in the inner ear give us our sense of balance and therefore undoubtedly play a role in our broader experience of symmetry and, in turn, rhythm—that is, of meanings suspended in equilibrium to create yet greater meanings.

Rhythm, as Katz points out, functions as a tacit, physical form of knowledge (107–108). In short, what Cicero, Isocrates, and others understood is that these stylistic devices are not merely *fun*, not just toys for writers, but tools by which writers can create certain effects on readers, physical feelings of comprehension and power, knowledge and connection. Careful rhythms and repetitions create, in a text, a latticework of interconnected moments, and this burgeoning bubble of "now" can, when one inhabits it, give rise to parallel experiences of connection between reader and writer and spark powerful acts of intuition that feel like the substance of knowledge itself. This intersubjective experience, which teachers call clarity, connects the writer's self with the Other, with that which, as such, has no clearly defined, easily controlled boundaries. In its profoundest instances, these are experiences of the infinite.

Unfortunately, this experience is often cast in naïve, popular discussions as liberation or, more vulgarly, self-indulgence. Or, just as bad, we strive to safeguard against these pleasures by reducing the whole domain of style to a set of tedious little exercises. Historically, however, the dominant metaphor for authorial pleasure, as I noted in the first chapter, is magic. Even today, when writers feel that their work is proceeding smoothly and spontaneously and in a way that feels readily readable, many of them will refer lightheartedly to the occult power of "the muse." Such remarks, though seemingly quite casual, actually embed a profound assertion about authorial pleasure. For example, in a chapter of *Writing with Power* called "Writing and Magic," Elbow notes that when our writing lacks magic, this absence is manifest in "little tell-tale movements in the body that somehow manifest discomfort" and "there are comparable micro-fidgets in our syntax and diction" (366–67). In other words, if the absence of "magic" leads to a flustered, uncomfortable experience of the composing process and a composition that is itself characterized by "micro-fidgets," then magic connotes the opposite: a pleasurable experience of composing and a composition that is comparatively more pleasurable (less "fidgety") for the reader. The experience of "magic" is the experience of pleasure in composing, but not just the pleasure of the writer alone: somehow, it is the pleasure of sharing pleasure with the Other, a quasi-erotic contact with that which is beyond the author. And, importantly, it registers in the text as the absence of "micro-fidgets in our syntax and diction." In short, it registers as highly disciplined style. Indeed, stylistic techniques provide the conduit between self and other. They create and sustain the moment of contact, of connection, of "clarity," in which the remarks of the author are renewed, made to "come alive" once again for the reader. This is the magical appearance of the muse as a textual bridge between author and audience and between past and future, a dissolution of the boundaries between them, an apotheosis of what hooks calls "the infinite."

While issues of the magical and the infinite might seem awfully exotic from the perspective of the workaday realities of the contemporary composition classroom, and while the preceding discussion might seem, theoretically, too abstract and, historically, too remote to have any meaningful bearing on practical matters of how we teach, I've developed some quite simple strategies for bringing my students to share in these considerable powers.

But How Do You Teach This Stuff?

On the first day of class, I distribute to my students a handout with the heading "Stylistic Devices" that begins this way:

> What follows is a list of verbal patterns or forms or "tricks" that you can use to make your prose more graceful, more powerful, and more memorable. Think of them, on one hand, as ornaments, as means to take what you've said and recast it in ways that your readers will enjoy. On the other hand, working with these forms can also stimulate your imagination—that is, as you work to reshape certain moments in your paper to fit these formulae, you may find all sorts of new ideas popping up.
>
> These devices are quite powerful. They were first organized more than two thousand years ago in ancient Greece, and they have had an overwhelming influence on the ways we've used language ever since. I've taken most of the information that follows from Richard Lanham's book *A Handlist of Rhetorical Terms*, where you'll find dozens upon dozens more such devices.
>
> Don't be intimidated or put off by the exotic names for these devices. Whether you learn to pronounce or spell these names correctly is not what's important. Also, don't feel as though you have to memorize them: at no point in the semester will you take a quiz or an exam in which you have to define each of these terms. Instead, simply try to become comfortable with these devices as tools that can give you more and more control over your prose, and, in turn, more and more success communicating with your readers. Remember, you should try to use at least two of these when you write your short homework papers, and, what's more, you will be required to use eight of them in your longer essay assignments.
>
> One last point by way of introduction, one that's *very, very important:* don't get hung up trying to fulfill these formulae before you know what you want to say! Rather, after you've done some brainstorming and have a general sense of the ideas and details you want to engage in your paper, then—and only then—should you start trying to make certain moments in your paper fulfill some of these

formulae. On the other hand, you might find that if you can't come up with ideas that you need for your paper, playing around with some of these devices can help generate ideas for writing. But only think of them this way when the brainstorming process feels genuinely stuck or blocked.

What follows is a list of some thirty terms. The first one is *accumulatio*, and I present it this way:

ACCUMULATIO (ak kyu myoo la TEE o): The heaping up of terms of praise or condemnation to summarize the points you've made. It works especially well in the conclusion of your paper. Example: "Thus, we see that Mayor Smith has been arrogant, uninformed, disloyal, greedy, deceitful, unreliable, and destructive."

The thirty or so terms end up with *zeugma;* I define and illustrate each one in a few short sentences (see the appendix for a copy of my most recent version of this handout, which has been expanded considerably). Initially, these terms were a little intimidating to students, and many of them felt, at the outset, that my requiring them to use these devices seemed incredibly difficult, even "a real pain in the neck."

To rescue my students from what they might otherwise view as an arduous, alienating, even pointless set of requirements, I began by explaining that what I want them to learn is something that, historically, has been thought of as magic. By using such a frankly silly-seeming term in the otherwise solemn context of the academy, I manage to lessen my students' feelings of intimidation and quicken their interest. I tell my students that I'm *not* talking about magic in the literal sense of ESP or levitating objects or rain dances. Rather, I'm talking about using symbols, not to fly in the face of the laws of nature and rationality, but rather to produce dramatic effects in the people around us. In this sense, the concept of magic applies to stunning works of art that change the way people think about their lives, deeply moving sermons or political speeches that prompt people to action, even great athletic performances that bring fans together and alter the ways people imagine the human body and its potentials.

I draw on William Covino (1994) and Kenneth Burke (1945) to say that what I'm interested in here is *generative magic* rather than *arresting magic*. The latter is a kind of lockstep incantation that is the opposite of critical and creative thinking. An example of arresting magic in the classroom would be the widespread belief of many students that fully formed texts simply spring forth from writers, effortlessly and inexplicably, like rabbits out of hats (see Young 1982). This arresting magic, too, is what Paulo Freire has in mind when he describes the mesmerized passivity and abject resignation of illiterate peasants, for arresting magic is employed by those at the center of mass culture to dazzle and coerce yet further those whom they dominate: it diminishes the masses' sense of choices and options, and, in turn, any experience of their own power and knowledge. Examples of arresting magic can be culled, as Covino points out, from the headlines of any of the supermarket tabloids: *Amazing New UFO Diet—Shed Pounds While You Sleep; Ten Steps to a Hotter Marriage; Get Rich the Easy Way With Trump's Simple Plan*. This sort of magic, as I said, is the opposite of the generative magic that, I hope, comes to permeate my classroom.

Magic in the generative sense is the mysterious power that drives the play of language. Generative magic can be cultivated by writers who, as Covino puts it, learn to serve as "assistants to the [generative] magic of words causing words," (1994, 92) who learn how, as Kenneth Burke puts it, to use those moments when "the act of writing brings up problems and discoveries intrinsic to the act, leading to developments . . . purely from the foregoing aspects of the act itself" (1945, 67). This mysterious playfulness that inheres in strings of words and causes them to yield more words, as Covino argues, "enlarges the grounds for action by the creation of choices"; because it creates choices, it in turn gives way to inward dialogue and reflection and then precipitates critique and judgement, which, as decisions are made, yield creative synthesis and commitment (1994, 26).

To cultivate generative magic, writers must learn techniques and principles that, rather than arrest the play of critical thought, stimulate it, structures that liberate rather than merely limit the composing imagination. These techniques allow the writer to cultivate that mysterious playfulness by which writing begets more writing and summons with keen temporal immediacy—just as speech does—responses from audiences.

When I introduce my students to these stylistic devices, I explain that my goal is not simply to get them to produce heavily stylized language, such as we might find in the Bible or Shakespeare, but rather to practice these devices as a kind of interim measure toward listening to and thinking about their prose more carefully. I think these devices achieve this end quite well. For example, one of my recent students, Elizabeth Sosa, told me that her previous schooling had instilled in her the habit of approaching writing assignments recklessly: "I would just put down any words that came to me without thinking about them at all till my paper was as long as it needed to be." But after just a few weeks of engaging these stylistic devices, she said, "I've changed. These devices force me to actually think about what I'm saying, rather than just putting down whatever." What I think is happening in Elizabeth's case, and in the case of many of my students, is that making use of these stylistic devices leads them to write with a greater degree of inward reflection, a heightened interaction with what Sondra Perl calls "the felt sense"(1980).

As my students struggle to use the stylistic devices, they constantly must ask themselves if a particular phrasing makes sense, if it feels right, or whether perhaps it feels like a problem, a snag in their attempts to communicate. Over the course of the semester, my students become increasingly familiar with the felt sense of communicative effectiveness, increasingly able to draw upon this "soft underbelly of thought . . . [this] bodily awareness" (Perl 1980, 363). The felt sense, they come to see, is a crucial tool for all writers. As Perl writes, "When we write and the writing is going well, we can tell by how we feel. This is not a purely mental or logical knowing but a bodily one." And she adds, "At such times we may feel a quickening and a sense of expansion or relief. But the reverse is also true. When the writing is not going well, we know it. We don't like how the words sound" (1994, 81). My students' use of these stylistic devices led them to interact with and learn to use the felt sense to increasing degrees over the course of the semester, and, as they did, they seemed to feel less alienated from the scene of writing, more happy to meet the challenges I set before them. They discovered the felt sense, in fact, as if it were something quite new, quite exciting, something they could cultivate and renew on an ongoing basis.

Given that Perl first introduced this concept of the felt sense in 1980, many teachers of writing have probably associated it with the expressivist idea of the authentic, personal voice, and, as such, it very likely ran afoul of the social-constructionist trend then beginning to move toward ascendance. The felt sense, however, despite its obvious resonance with popular concepts of so-called gut instinct, also can be thought of as something like an "audience-within," a receptor or interlocutor we carry in our musculature and that tells us if we're writing well or not. The felt sense also functions much the same way that the collective encyclopedia functioned in the ancient rhapsodes. "The felt sense," as Perl quotes Eugene Gendlin, "encompasses everything you feel and know about a given subject at given time" (1980, 115). It is not therefore a private space, a space of purest subjectivity or self-expression, not the "real me" or "my true voice," but just the opposite: the felt sense is the domain of the transpersonal, the point of contact with the Other. In this light, learning to "get in touch" with the felt sense means learning to connect with the surrounding community, learning to overcome alienation and master strategies for meeting audiences. When students play around with ways of patterning sentences in a given passage, this activity not only triggers new ideas for writing, but, at the same time, it also enables them to get a feel for what sounds best in a given moment in their prose and a feel for the generative magic by which words beget more words. Their pleasure, I believe, is a residue of the ecstasy of the ancient rhapsodes.

In fact, my students manifest a quite stunning sort of energy when I link these stylistic devices, explicitly, to exercises with the felt sense. Early in the semester, as was the case with Elizabeth, they wanted to "hurry up and get it over with," putting down words fairly thoughtlessly to bring the anxious experience of the composing process to a quick, sloppy end. And so, they initially resisted these devices. In order to diminish their sense of the sheer hassle of dealing with language as carefully as I required, I devoted a class meeting to helping them rethink, through the felt sense and through a stylistic device known as *chiasmus*, their recently completed rough drafts. I had assigned my students a topic that required them to synthesize ideas in essays by Alice Walker and Nancy Mairs on the dynamics of body image and the practice of writing and to use this connection as the springboard for their own thoughts on what role writing can play in the struggle to cultivate what the students had come to call, through our class discussions, "inner beauty." We had had several great discussions, most of which I had ended by asking my students to freewrite, so they would have plenty of raw material from which to create a draft. On the day the first drafts were due, I told them that today there would be no discussion, that instead, I wanted to ask them a series of questions about their drafts and that they should write the answers out in their notebooks.

I told them first to read through their drafts once, straight through, without pausing to make any changes. Once they had finished, I asked each of them to write a paragraph on how they felt about the draft. I gave them a few minutes, and then asked a question that probed a little more deeply: "What moment in your essay is the smartest, the most impressive? Why?" I then asked a couple of questions designed to promote a certain kind of free-association that would lead to the felt sense. "Can you," I asked, "link this moment to a particular person or place or event? If you already have made a connection to one of these in your paper, try to link it to one of the others, to something that is not, at present, in your paper." I then asked them, "What emotions do you associate with this connection?" And then, after a minute or two, "Suppose, for the time being, that an emotion is really something like a half-formed thought, an incomplete thought, something you know but that you don't realize that you know—yet. What message or information might be hiding inside the emotion that you've mentioned?" I then told them to freewrite and develop this idea for five minutes.

Next, I said, "Now, read back over what you just wrote. Can you boil it down to a sort of basic opposition, something like *X versus Y*?" I gave them some time to think, and then I said, "Now, try putting the two terms of this conflict together under a single label, a label that pins down not their opposition, but the connection between them, the thing they share." Again, I gave them some time to think and said, "Now that you've got this term that binds them together, jot down what you think might be the opposite of this term." I then asked them to retrace these steps and come up with a sentence in which the two key terms of the first half of the sentence were repeated in reverse order in the second half. That is, I asked them to create a chiasmus, something like "Ask not what your country can do for you, but what you can do for your country." The steps I had just led them through by no means could automatically yield a chiasmus, but I hoped that, by helping them to think in terms of oppositions and multiple levels of generalization, I could get them moving toward one.

Needless to say, they struggled. After a few minutes, though, several of them were ready to share their attempts, and, as we jostled these examples to fit the form, more of the students began to catch on. The students soon began to bring an extraordinary energy to this task, and this energy accumulated in intensity as they competed with each other to engineer a chiasmus. One student, Jessi Courville, said that working on her chiasmus was triggering so many new ideas and possibilities for her paper that she felt as if her mind was about to "boil over." As she said this, she was beaming. Nearly everyone in the class became increasingly animated as we worked on shaping their assertions into a chiasmus: hardly the ecstasy of the ancient rhapsodes, but certainly something bordering on its elusive descendant, that strange sensation that we've traditionally called inspiration or magic.

One student raised his hand and read his sentence: "The question, ultimately, is this: does having a keen sense of your own inner beauty turn you into a writer, or does writing on a regular basis give you a keen sense of your own inner beauty? In other words, the question of beauty and becoming a writer is just like the question of the chicken and the egg. It's impossible to say which comes first and causes the other." Another student wrote, "If you can master your feelings about the issue of external beauty, you will be beautiful, but if questions about external beauty master you, you will be ugly. Writing can help the inner defeat the outer, but advertising and the media can help the outer defeat the inner."

Most of the others weren't quite as good, but my students found that, in spite of the difficulty of creating a chiasmus, the struggle itself was producing lots of new ideas and details that they could include in their essays. What's more, the students seemed to be having fun, and the work they produced was certainly fun to read: when I looked at their next drafts, the writing was indeed richer and more complex than most freshman writing I'm used to seeing.

The chief flaw in my students' drafts at this stage was that they often dropped the stylistic figures into their papers pretty much at random.

Those examples of chiasmus, above, might appear virtually anywhere in the essay, and, as I discussed the students' drafts with them, nearly all of them reported that, despite the power of the stylistic devices to generate ideas, the devices' placement in the finished product was not so much due to careful reflection but rather to chance or random opportunity. The figures could just as easily appear in the middle of a paragraph somewhere toward the middle of the essay as in the introduction or conclusion, and they could be used to express minor details or major themes. In other words, the devices seemed to destabilize, sometimes quite drastically, their experience of the overall structure of the essay.

After looking at their drafts and considering the problem, I decided to help them situate this sense of the architecture of individual sentences within the larger architecture of the entire essay. Borrowing from Joseph Williams (1981), I introduced them to four stylistic principles that the class came to identify, respectively, as "focus," "flow," "story," and "rhythmic emphasis" (again, see the appendix for the handout that describes these principles for my students).

In short, "focus" is the idea that, within each paragraph, each sentence should begin with a topic that fits with the other topics of the other sentences in that paragraph. If these topics, together, form a consistent string, then the paragraph is well focused; that is, if the topic of several sentences in a row is "I" but then a fifth sentence in the paragraph sets forth, as its topic, the words *pickup truck*, then, right there, at *pickup truck*, the focus has begun to blur. The same principle that can help writers focus individual paragraphs can be used to focus an entire essay: that is, if the topic of each paragraph throughout the essay makes a consistent set, then the paper is well focused, but if one paragraph suddenly begins with a reference that seems unrelated to the openings of the other paragraphs that precede and that follow it, then the essay's focus, at exactly that moment, has temporarily wobbled or even gone entirely off track.

Much like the principle of "focus," I explained to them that the principle of "flow" allows writers to reflect in fairly objective ways on how readers will experience their prose. Very simply, if each sentence begins with a word, phrase, or concept that, within the immediate context, is familiar to the reader, and if the sentence then ends with material that is not familiar, then readers will find that the sentence flows smoothly and will proceed along to the next sentence without stumbling.

I then told my students about a principle that is closely related to these concepts, an idea we came to call, in shorthand, the idea of "story." I suggested that the human mind seems to have a relatively easy time engaging information when that information is organized at least in part as a story. That is, we like to organize information in terms of characters and the actions they perform. This dynamic of character and action (that is, story) accounts for why our sentences usually must have a subject (character) and a verb (action) in order to really engage the reader. Moreover, the sooner within the sentence that writers deliver what readers most want—a subject followed very closely by a verb—the more readily will those readers engage the writer's sentences.

I was careful not to overwhelm the students by introducing them to these ideas all at once. Rather, I took up only one per class meeting, provided many examples, and gave the students time in class to tinker with moments in their drafts according to these ideas. I constantly reminded them that they should always have these principles in mind when they were revising their work, especially when they were working with a stylistic device.

This concept of "story" connects well with another concept for revising their essays and connecting with readers, the idea of rhythmic emphasis. This, I told them, is one of the most important features of successful prose. Of course, prose style is way too complicated a subject to allow for any sort of simplistic definition of its rhythm. Nonetheless, I drew again from Joseph Williams a way of tinkering with individual sentences to give them rhythmic emphasis, and this idea, especially when coupled with the previous idea of story, can make sentences more engaging for readers. Consider the fact, I told them, that when a reader reads a sentence out loud, his or her voice nearly always rises and falls toward the ends of sentences. "Try it yourself," I said, "you can hear your voice naturally rise and fall on the last word or two of a sentence as you stress one syllable more strongly than you do the others, like this—listen—'more strongly than you do the OTH-ers.'" I told them that same thing happens even when one is reading silently—that is, the rhythmic rise and fall is registered in the felt sense. And therefore, given that the ends of sentences are always places where we naturally expect to hear a certain dramatic rise and fall, we should only put words at the end of our sentences that are quite important—that is, words or phrases that are worthy of this special, rhythmic thrust.

I remind my students, again and again, that this principle of rhythmic emphasis should be exercised in a delicate balance with the idea of story. That is, the character and action of a sentence/story are certainly important, even essential, but so much so that they are often understood by readers, sentence by sentence, as a kind of "given," and what's most important of all, where the real drama of a sentence/story lurks, is in the effect or result of the character's action, and that's why that material should come in the place of greatest rhythmic emphasis, the sentence's end. This formula is hardly as tired and lockstep as the five-paragraph theme and is, in fact, flexible enough to keep the students from falling into a rote method. Above all, it gives them a larger framework within which to imagine using particular stylistic devices, preventing them from suffering the completely open-ended sense that these devices can be randomly dropped into the text anywhere without careful attention to context or timing.

In the broadest sense, these devices and principles sensitize my students to how their readers experience their prose. In addition to structuring the work of revision and lending that potentially open-ended process a comforting set of priorities and a "to-do list," it awakens my students to the fact that reading too is, for readers, always a process, a sequence of moments that good writers know how to choreograph. In short, these devices allow my students to start playing around with the experience of time: if the principle of flow, for example, is observed rigorously, the essay will seem to move forward very quickly, but if it is troubled slightly, the essay will slow down, and certain dramatic, abrupt figures like the chiasmus can draw enough attention to themselves to stop, temporarily, the forward movement of the essay altogether. This power to manipulate time can feel magical and it derives directly from a keen, imaginative interaction with the reader.

Scarcely more than a month into the semester, my students began to report that working with the stylistic devices was getting easier and even downright fun, like playing a game. And so I thought about trying to cultivate this energy, to sensitize them yet further to style as a tool for the pleasurable experience of connecting with others. More and more often, I would ask students to read out loud so they could come to see the way patterns of stress interact with patterns of meaning (see Katz 1996). Whenever I did, I thought about Richard Lanham's idea (1983) that when we read out loud, we instantly radicalize the latent, social dimension of the text in ways that silent reading suppresses: that is, we evince an attitude toward it, and, beyond it, we set forth a web of emotionally nuanced relationships between ourselves, our immediate surroundings, the people who can hear us, and the text. I encouraged my students to note the ways reading out loud makes us take a stand and put ourselves on the line, activating the relations between self, text, and world in ways that are quite energizing (1983, 105). In the terms I've been using, this energizing effect—this pleasure—stems from the experience of reimmersion in community, in the realm of lived connections and consequences. Indeed, when called upon to read aloud, students often initially resist, for it throws into play all sorts of processes that, as I argued in the first chapter, they are programmed to lock down or sidestep.

In addition to thinking about reading out loud, I began to think about a technique I heard about several years ago in which students memorize and recite randomly chosen paragraphs from their papers.

We always find it nearly impossible to memorize something that we don't find particularly meaningful or involving, but the opposite sort of language is quite easy to memorize. Should I, I asked myself, revive that old "memorization test"? Rather than actually assign it, I mentioned it, as a possibility, to my students, something I might offer to them as a chance for extra credit or as one aspect of a revision project.

I tried other assignments to promote the kind of inward reflection about language that I'd been advocating since the beginning of the semester. Here is the topic of the third major writing assignment I gave them:

> Powerful endings characterize all four of the essays we've recently read, and all four of these endings seem to use a powerful symbolic object: in Andee Hochman's essay, "Growing Pains," there is the grandmother's wedding ring; in E. B. White's essay, "Once More to the Lake," there is the son's cold, soggy swimming suit; in Natalie Kusz's essay, "Ring Leader," there is the nose-ring; and in the article from *Adbusters,* there is the reference to billboards.
>
> On the other hand, each of these endings is very different. That is, each has a very different tone, a very different mood, and these varying moods are achieved through very different writing styles, different devices. Study these essays closely, and then contrast the endings to any two of them.
>
> Specifically, consider the differences in tone and how the tone is achieved through particular verbal techniques.
>
> You'll certainly want to consider the issue of "focus" in the essays' final passages. What is the dominant focus on and why? Are there any abrupt shifts? If so, what would make these disruptions appropriate to the mood the writer is creating and the theme s/he is addressing? Ask yourself the same kinds of questions about "flow." Does the final passage of the text move very quickly? That is, does the final passage of a particular essay observe the principle of flow very strictly or does it wind down with a deliberate sort of stumbling that helps to enhance the particular mood or tone of the passage? Are there other ways to talk about how the essay works with and against the principles of focus and flow?
>
> Also, you'll want to consider what sorts of stylistic devices the authors use and what sorts of effects these devices have. That is, how do they contribute to the mood of the ending? Important note: sometimes, authors do not use a stylistic device with absolute accuracy but rather choose to employ a slightly looser version of the device to make it fit more smoothly. Therefore, as you notice and comment on certain features of the essay's endings, be open to the idea that the devices aren't necessarily used with perfect exactitude.
>
> What about the issue of rhythmic emphasis? How does the writer work with and against the idea that readers expect to find the words of greatest importance in the position of the sentence that has the

greatest rhythmic emphasis—that is, the sentence's end. What is the effect of the author's choices regarding this issue? How do these choices contribute to the mood of the ending?

What else can you say about the voice or tone or mood of the endings? Of the two you're comparing, which is more powerful and why? Remember, this is not a question about the content of the essay, but about *how the endings sound*. Therefore, avoid mere summary of the author's ideas.

Additional Requirement: Use any eight stylistic devices.

Extra Credit: Try to end your essay in a way that closely imitates the endings of one of the essays we've read. That is, give your sentences essentially the same structure and tone. If you try to do this, let me know with a short note at the bottom of the page: tell me whom you're imitating and how you went about it.

My students claimed that this was one of the toughest paper topics they had ever seen. Nonetheless, several of them handled it extremely well. After they handed in their rough drafts, I photocopied a relatively typical paper, distributed it to the class, and we worked on revising it together. After working on this revision as a group, I encouraged them to use the paper as a model as they revised their own essays. Here is the original draft of the paper, complete with the numbers indicating which stylistic devices were used, as noted at the end of the paper:

Mood Creating Techniques
By Robert Tillman

The essays of Andee Hochman and E. B. White use very clever ways of creating a mood or tone for their works. They use contrasting methods to manipulate tones, tones they derive from the use of the different elements of focus, flow, emphasis, and stylistic devices (#1). This manipulation occurs through the ways in which such devices, as well as common text, are positioned. Positioning has everything to do with reaching the desired effect, whether it is creating a piece that flows well to create a sense of calm or confidence or not following focus or flow very carefully to slow the essay down or to create a sense of confusion. Well positioned stylistic devices are not only essential for determining mood, but also engage the reader on a more profound level (#2).

The primary difference in the endings of the essays by Andee Hochman and E. B. White is that Hochman is focused on the confusion she feels and White is bringing about a sense of death. Hochman's confusion is personified through her stylistic use of her grandmother's ring. The ring symbolizes the image of her family that she has had to break away from by coming out as a lesbian. The use of the ring is strategically placed in the ending of the essay to provide the sense of the superficial relationship with her family so that she may be truthful with them and herself. Hochman's relationship to her family can be salvaged if her parents put aside the perfect family image that no family can truthfully live up to.

You can really get a feel for the confusion Hochman is experiencing by paying attention to the text. In the final paragraphs of the text she puts out a feeling of extreme self-absorption through her increased use of the word "I." This usage shows the reader that by using rapid flow with "I," she cannot break away from her own mind and the thoughts that proceed from it. The aforementioned confusion is further exemplified by Hochman's questioning herself shown through the quote, "Were my relatives still there with their shopping and their sweaters, their softening faces and their stiff resistance to change? If I returned, would I be swallowed up? If I stayed, would I be left adrift? Is that the brittle choice that, ultimately, forms the boundary line of every family: Be like us or be alone?" This quote is the most powerful one of the two essays because it is an excellent example of the stylistic device, epiplexis. She uses this questioning manner to attack herself. Hochman is able to sum up all her feelings and summarize the mood of the essay in a few short sentences, the last of which is most intriguing. "Alone" is the final word of the paragraph and is a great representation of emphasis. Being alone with herself is what she is struggling with, bringing back to light the rapid flow using the word "I," not being able to break away from the oppressive thoughts her mind is putting out.

She made up her mind to come out of the closet to her family and in effect break the perfect family image and consequently separate herself from her relatives. Hochman discovered that the important part of life is not to falsely appear happy, but to be truthful to yourself and others (#3). This is supported by her losing the image in the ring which was a symbol of the family bond, in essence leaving behind her family which would rather keep up the false image of normalcy. This bond was further interrupted by her moving to the other side of the country and stopping her work as a more socially respected journalist to a less respected street youth counselor. Taking up this line of work was yet another device that Hochman used to show that she was going to do what made her feel happy.

Happiness, however, would still be a ways away because she was still torn between herself and her family. This is shown in the last two paragraphs of the essay by again using rapid flow with the word "I," but then interrupting this smoothness by breaking the flow with quotes that slow down the flow greatly by beginning sentences on unfamiliar ground. Either these quotes are meant to create their own degree of confusion or she unwittingly made a great statement (#4). Hochman arranges these quotes in a manner that directly contradict one another. She puts, "You can do anything you sent your mind to" just before "Don't leave." She also adds, "Follow your dreams" ahead of "Stay put." These quotes may seem out of place by themselves, but when considered with the rest of the ending they serve as a great technique for mood resonance (#5).

Hochman is able to arrange these quotes and the entire ending of the essay in a manner that creates a lot of friction. Friction and confusion, used in the right manner, are not detrimental (#6). Hochman's use of well-structured confusion presents an important stylistic device (#7). Using style in this way is excellent because it reflects perfectly the mood of the essay. The mood is conveyed through her use of rapid flow which is broken by a much slower one, a key placing of the stylistic device epiplexis, a strong usage of emphasis and some important contradicting quotes.

However, E. B. White's essay conveys a much different focus. He uses his techniques to confront readers with a morbid tone, one of death. With death being such a powerful word, it is no wonder why White would put as much emphasis on it as that last word entails. The last sentence of the essay goes, "As he buckled the swollen belt, suddenly my groin felt the chill of death." This "chill of death" goes much deeper than his groin. Ever since he made his long awaited return to the cabin, this time with his own son, he has been getting the sensation that his son is now him, and he his father (#8).

White uses this sensation to relate his experience to the circle of life. Part of the circle of life is the new replacing of the old, such as him replacing his father. This is also implied through the replacing of the older soft drinks with Coca Cola and the outboard boat motors replacing the older ones. The switching out of old and new is not White's focus though. He focuses on the final part of life instead.

A feeling of death is encased in the final paragraphs of his essay. Death is personified through the thunderstorm. He builds up to it by using words such as "the big scene" and "the whole thing." These are meant to get the reader thinking of the big picture, sort of looking back on everything before death, the thunderstorm sets in. Then you have "a curious darkening of the sky," and a "lull in everything that made life tick." This can be seen as the slowing of the vital signs. Then you have death itself with "the gods grinning and licking their chops in the hills." The flow is also interrupted at this point by changing to writing of drums, which is symbolic of life being interrupted by death. Death is also showing up in the quote "the turtles slid off of the sunny logs and dug their way into the soft bottom." They are burying themselves.

White is seeing all these signs of death on a subconscious level until the final sentence when he finally realizes it and feels the chill of death when his son puts on his wet bathing suit. He is able to bring these revelations to the readers by his use of the techniques of flow and emphasis.

#1 Anadiplosis
#2 Dirimens Copulatio
#3 Syncresis
#4 Disjunctive Proposition
#5 Antanagoge

#6 Litotes
#7 Oxymoron
#8 Zeugma

As a class, we worked through this paper, sentence by sentence, paragraph by paragraph, talking about what could be improved. I first put the students in small groups, made each group responsible for discussing a particular paragraph in the paper, and, after about ten minutes, returned them all to large-group discussion. The class quickly pointed out that Rob's discussion of symbols—the jewelry, the swimming suit—was not important and should be cut. One group worried about Rob starting the third paragraph with the word "you," because the focus of that paragraph is not on the reader. They added that while the paragraph flowed well, its focus could be tighter, especially toward the end. One sentence, they pointed out, began with the word "alone," which doesn't fit at all with the topics of the other sentences in the paragraph ("she," "usage," "confusion," "quote," "she," and "Hochman"). The string of topics, they said, could be tightened a little, and the sentence that began with "alone" really needed to be rethought.

Another group made similar remarks about the next paragraph: the flow is great, they said, but the focus could be tighter, especially toward the end where that last sentence begins "Taking up this line of work . . ." At this point, another group chimed in with an exciting discovery: "You know, the same things happen in the paragraph we worked on—the flow is great, but the focus breaks up toward the end." One of the students directed everyone's attention to the second-to-last paragraph, saying, "Look at the string of topics—it goes, 'a feeling of death,' 'death,' 'he,' 'these,' you,' 'this,' 'the flow,' 'death,' 'they.'" I asked the student what she made of this, and she answered, "Well, the focus mostly sticks to the word *death*, except right before the end where there's 'you,' 'this,' and 'flow.' Rob should tighten up that ending." The student then added, "And he should watch out for the endings of all of his paragraphs, because he has a tendency to lose his focus a little at that point."

Another student said, "But maybe that's part of the mood Rob is trying to create in the paper, a mood of constantly breaking out to deal with new stuff." The class argued back and forth about whether or not this was, in fact, a useful tone to adopt and whether or not Rob had achieved it, and so on.

My students seemed to love this discussion, and a couple of them explicitly mentioned that they felt newly enabled to revise their own essays—a task that, before class, they had been dreading. One of them, Starr Moffett, sent me a note about the assignment as a whole: "A great mix of challenge, hard work, and pure interest made this paper a joy to do." And she added that she was "fired up" to start revising. Part of what seemed to energize my students was the work of constantly rereading parts of Rob's paper out loud as we discussed its style and sought to ascertain its strengths and weaknesses.

The Writer's Double

Teaching students to play with stylistic devices and encouraging them to read out loud are part of the broad project of helping them to develop a sense of audience and engage in inward dialogue, critical reflection, and generative "magic." In other words, the trick of writing well has a great deal to do, as Walter Ong notes in "The Writer's Audience Is Always a Fiction" (1975, 1997), with one's ability to create and manage not just certain local effects on the audience but also a kind of consistent, global *role* for that audience. One can then put one's self in the position of that audience and reread one's work to look for moments when that audience might stumble. Much the same point occasions Joseph Williams' practical book on style (2000), which is organized around a list of ten highly flexible principles for considering one's prose from a reader's point of view and for revising it to ensure as much as possible that one's readers will have the experience one wants them to have.

All writers, Ong suggests, instinctively try to do this whenever they write. For example, when a student is faced with the problem of writing a paper for a teacher, he or she will likely muddle around trying to get a draft going, but no draft will begin to emerge until the student discovers how he or she wants to sound. Suppose the student has read *The Adventures of Tom Sawyer*. The student, says Ong, "knows what this book felt like, how the voice in it addressed its readers." And so the student supposes, "Why not pick up that voice and, with it, its audience? Why not make like Samuel Clemens and write for whomever Samuel Clemens was writing for?" (1975, 59). The student is instinctively playing on a particular strand in her partial version of the collective encyclopedia, her felt sense, one roughly labeled "Clemens," in the hopes that the patterns of that particular strand will serve to engage the reader the same way it so memorably did for her when she read Clemens' work. The student intuitively understands that if she does a fairly good job of imitating Clemens and if the teacher has no great problem playing the role of the Clemens-reader, then the paper is likely to be thought of as very "clear" and to earn a good grade. But what if the teacher finds such a voice either corny or stilted or arcane—what then? The student will have to redraft and, this time, she will have to adopt some other writer's methods for constructing the reader's role. What makes this task of inward dialogue so difficult is that there are no hard-and-fast rules or directives that one can memorize and repeat to govern what is, after all, an endlessly nuanced, almost molecular sort of connection between reader and writer.

A point much like Ong's was made some two decades ago by Donald Murray. "The act of writing," he says, "might be described as a conversation between two workmen, muttering to each other at the workbench." He explains, "The self speaks, the other self listens and responds. The self proposes, the other self evaluates. The two selves collaborate" (1982, 140). What these two workmen mutter about is words and how it feels to use one rather than another, as well as phrases and their arrangement, and how one sequence rather than an alternate might sound better, might more fully connect with a particular audience. This second self, this internalized or imagined audience, is very much akin to what Havelock would call, in the context of the ancient rhapsodes, the collective, Homeric encyclopedia. To define it phenomenologically, I think we might characterize this special zone or force as something that writers can cultivate in much the same way that Elbow asks us to cultivate "speech." Like speech, like Perl's felt sense, it is dialogic, full of spontaneity, contextual immediacy, and rhythmic thrust. Whether we call it by any of these names or by *kairos* or timing or sound, we must surely agree that increasing sensitivity to it plays an invaluable role in the development of the student writer.

And, regrettably, this Other-within, as some have pointed out, is becoming more and more elusive, more and more difficult to contact. As Lynn Worsham puts it, this Other-within can harden into the sort of authority that blocks expression. That is, it can become "disembodied and abstract," but, once the student embraces it, she says, it can form the necessary rallying point for critical reflection (1991, 142). As I argued toward the end of the first chapter, I think precisely this sort of block characterizes many students: they have, as Mike Rose might put it, internalized a conglomeration of half-understood but wholly inflexible rules, ideals, and goals that form a kind of buttress against the lived experience of the processes of thinking, writing, and learning, a firewall against the very inspiring, even bodily experience of awakening literacy (1980).

At the risk of waxing nostalgic for a Golden Age that most likely never was, my dream is help students dismantle this modern firewall, to become what Jean Baudrillard (1993) calls "primitives." The primitive subject, according to Baudrillard, differs from the modern subject, first, because the primitive is suffused with pleasure, whereas the modern is fundamentally alienated and anxiety-stricken. The primitives experience pleasure because they have a relationship with a "double," whereas the anxiety-stricken moderns have internalized an abstract agency or idealized some dogmatic code that alienates them from their doubles. Between the primitive and the double, says Baudrillard, "there is neither a mirror relation nor one of abstraction, as there is between the subject and its spiritual principle, the soul, or between the subject and its moral or psychological principle, consciousness" (141). What, then, is this double? The double is not simply a repetition of one's self, not the "true self" of so-called expressivism nor a mirror image of one's ego, but simply an Other-within, one of a potentially vast horde of such doubles that one can conjure into dialogue. According to Baudrillard, the double is "an invisible part" of the self, a "partner with whom the primitive . . . has a certain type of visible exchange" via words, symbols, or gestures (141). This relation with the double, though "sometimes happy, sometimes not," is implicitly pleasurable, says Baudrillard, for its failure produces a profound anxiety. The double's erosion or complete disappearance occurs when one "internalizes an abstract agency . . . to which everything else is subordinated" (142). This is the advent of the "soul" or of "consciousness" (142), and with it the subject undergoes a very real confinement and separation, the worst sort of submission to mechanisms of social control. In short, one becomes "modern."

In the terms of the last chapter, the modern is a masochistic subject, one who has internalized and fetishized some ideal, a representation of the Law, before which one must grovel and quake in the hope of appeasement, or still worse, sit frozen in fear of its power to harm. Indeed, to the degree that we forfeit our relationship with our double, to the degree that we become "modern," we are plunged into profound anxiety and alienation. "[T]he things closest to us," Baudrillard writes, "such as our own bodies, the body itself, our voice and our appearance, are separated from us to the precise extent that we internalize the soul (or any other equivalent agency or abstraction)." To do so, adds Baudrillard, "kills off the proliferation of doubles and spirits, consigning them once again to the spectral, embryonic corridors of unconscious folklore, like the ancient gods that Christianity . . . transformed into demons" (142).

The modern world, argues Baudrillard, "is haunted by the spectres of these alienated doubles, creating anxiety that wells up around the most familiar things" (142). Surely, this anxiety imbues the situation of sitting down to write, for, when we must imagine an audience to address, we are trying to interact with a double whom we have lost. Re-accessing one's double—or, rather, doubles—means conjuring them from the "spectral embryonic corridors of unconscious folklore," where they have been consigned as "demons," and, as I argued in Chapter 1, the "demon" whom the modern conjures is that idealized vision of perfection, the humiliating dominatrix who binds and secures us against any arcs of becoming, who sows doubt and defeatism in us, and who compels us to refuse challenges and turn away from growth.

How do we recreate the primitive experience of the double? I think that the kinds of ideas I've offered in this chapter might point in the right direction, for Baudrillard says that to interact with doubles is "to speak to one's body and to speak to language" (141). In the more familiar words of composition theory, I think we might translate this as a suggestion that we can help students return to the more pleasurable, primitive position by constantly asking them to reflect on their prose style from the standpoint of their felt sense.

Many might object that the emphasis on prose style I've delineated in this chapter can lead—no matter how much I invoke the felt sense—only to an empty and deadening formalism that our students will find an absolute bore. Surely, they'll find no pleasure in writing unless the topic they're writing about has something to do with their own lives, their own ideas.

For example, when we were discussing their drafts for the essay in which students had to analyze the stylistic features of the concluding paragraphs of some of the essays we had been reading, the first question everyone wanted to raise was whether or not they could write about the tone of those endings by referring to their own personal experience of the ending. They kept asking, "Are we allowed to say, 'I feel that . . .' or 'My experience of this ending is . . .'"

Of course, my answer was yes. I was intrigued by their desire to take control over this daunting topic by connecting it to their own experience, so much so that I asked them how they might like to make more room in the next assignment topic for discussing their own experience. They responded in a general way by saying they didn't much care about how the assignment made this possibility available to them, just so long as the possibility was there. "All semester long," one of them said, "we've been writing about other writers," and, as the rest of the class nodded in agreement, the student went on, "so before the semester ends, can we please, please just write about ourselves." Many of those who had been nodding in agreement began to speak up: "Yeah, yeah, that would be good. We've done enough with the readings—let's just write about ourselves for once."

"All right," I said, "the last paper—which, as you know, has to be written in class—will be just about you."

They cheered.

And so, just before the last day of the semester, I gave them the following topic, and told them they would have a little less than an hour to write, and added that they could not bring notes or outlines to class that day. Normally, my students dread this particular requirement of my department's composition curriculum, but this time they seemed excited. I began the topic with two quotes from their fellow students that had appeared during a self-reflexive journal assignment I had given them a few weeks prior. In the next chapter, I'll explore their responses to this topic in the context of later versions of that renegade tradition in the history of rhetoric. Here's the topic:

> "Okay, this is going to sound like I'm a nerd, but I already think this class is fun."
>
> *—Starr Moffett*

> "I actually enjoyed linking the stylistic devices into my paper."
>
> *—Bradley Yee*

On Tuesday, April 30th, you will write a short paper in class. The paper should be roughly 500 words. Do not, however, waste valuable time counting the words—instead, before class that day, count how many words written in your own handwriting fill up a page and, from there, figure out how many pages you need to fill to create a long enough essay. Also, be sure to leave time at the end of the class period to proofread your work so no misspellings or grammatical errors disrupt the reader's experience of your paper.

As these two quotes from Starr and Bradley suggest, some people think that writing can be fun. What do you suppose are the crucial ingredients that make writing a pleasurable experience? If your experience this semester has differed significantly from that of Starr and Bradley, then attack their position: analyze how and why your own experience is so different, why their claims don't ring true. On the other hand, if you feel as though you can relate to their experience, then analyze this experience and explain what makes writing fun.

Three

Songs of Experience
A Stoic Cult of the Sublime and Today's Student of Style

According to the national school-based Youth Risk Behavior study, sponsored by the United States Centers for Disease Control, 27 percent of all high school students thought seriously about committing suicide in 1990; 8 percent of all high school students actually attempted suicide; and 2 percent of all students sustained injuries in the course of a suicide attempt serious enough to warrant medical attention. The study, which surveyed 11,631 high school students from every state in the country, estimated over a quarter of a million high school students made at least one suicide attempt requiring hospitalization in the preceding twelve months.

—Jeffrey Berman and
Jonathan Schiff, 2000

[T]hose of us whose professional lives are defined by the writing classroom often find ourselves reading essays that contain the traumatic life stories of our students, even when such stories are not the focus of the class or of the assignments we give.

—Charles Anderson and
Marian MacCurdy, 2000

My students' responses to that final, in-class essay have prompted me to expand my claims about what an immersion in style can offer a student writer and to articulate these expanded claims through further accounts of that renegade tradition in rhetoric. In fact, as I realized,

57

asking students to discuss their experience of writing can lead to powerful revelations. I had begun to sense, over the course of the semester, that while my students were put off, initially, by the requirement to use stylistic devices, their work with style had increasingly become a source of considerable pleasure. What's more, I began to notice dramatic improvements in their writing: their essays did indeed flow more smoothly and observe a tighter focus, both of which seemed to enable more complicated, more profound content. Perhaps most happily, their prose was characterized by increasing verve and adventure, more poetry and inspiration. For these reasons, and also in response to their pleading, I became particularly curious about how they were experiencing the work of composing essays for my class. Hence, that final, in-class essay topic. Nothing, however, quite prepared me for their responses.

I first began to wonder about the possibility of assigning such a topic when Ken Rayes, a colleague of mine in New Orleans, told me about a journal prompt he likes to use on the first day of the semester. In order to get a sense of how his students perceive writing and what role writing plays in their lives, he asks them to fill in the blanks in the following statement and then explain their choices: "If writing were a food, it would be [blank], because it [blank]." His students' responses, he says, generally fall into a few categories. The students most often say that writing is like a particular food that takes many steps to cook or create, or they'll say that it is like some food that blends a great many ingredients, or they'll compare it to an unusual food in order to make an assertion about the unpredictability of individual tastes. Sometimes, however, Ken gets responses that are rather startling. Here's one:

> I can enjoy a food, but I struggle for an essay, especially for English class. I don't know why when I face a blank piece of paper, I can barely move my pen without pondering. The more I ponder, the more I feel my head is number. Sometimes I have to take hours to finish an introduction of an essay. To me writing is never like food. It is like chewing on a rock.

I certainly wouldn't suppose that the sort of pedagogy outlined in the previous chapter could instantly fix the mind-numbing pain this student associates with writing. Nor could I hope to alleviate all of the agony and terror that my first epigraph for this chapter suggests is widespread among students taking freshman composition and that, as the second epigraph reminds us, frequently spills into their writing. Nonetheless, as I suggested earlier, by carefully considering the sorts of positive experiences our classrooms manage to precipitate, we can perhaps imagine ways to increase their frequency and to stave off the opposite sort of experience, the one in which writing an essay for school is like chewing on a rock.

Part of the difficulty of this project, however, is the possibility that, as many would surely point out, the pleasure my pedagogy seeks to foster is not quite the opposite of the pain it so much hopes to assuage. More specifically, the problem with pleasure as a classroom goal is that, for some students, the most pleasurable classroom experience they can imagine comes only when they express themselves most destructively: that is, when they confront the teacher or each other with a cruel sneer or when they masochistically turn that sneer inward to shut themselves down and short-circuit any intellectual adventures that could jeopardize their top priority, the securing of certain privileges within the status quo. For much these same reasons, perhaps, many teachers also distrust pleasure: too often, pleasure seems to run counter to our commitment to professionalism.

Although rhetoric's earliest interests revolved, as I noted, around the therapeutic power of words as "bearers of pleasure and banishers of pain," those who strove to explore and elaborate these possibilities were attacked, driven underground, and flagged as renegades and magicians by those who represented the authority of rationality. Whether merely silly or downright destructive, pleasure even today is cast as the opposite of what we value most. Again, as we saw, the most pleasure-centered of contemporary rhetorics, *écriture feminine*, is defined as pure excess or negativity, as that which can only antagonize the university. What this pattern implies, of course, is that because pleasure is so disruptive, the primary signature of serious professionalism can only be a grimace of pain.

Pain, perhaps, serves as a stabilizing, focusing, grounding force within and against the dizzying swirl of enticements and the constantly shifting social landscape that characterize consumer culture. In fact, pain would seem to fill the void created by the slide in our culture that Mark Edmundson describes: instead of searching for liberation and pleasure, as we did in the 1960s and '70s, we have in the decades since then reduced ourselves to an enthusiasm for mere buying power and the instant gratification of readily available commodities. If this enthusiasm's objects are as ephemeral and frivolous as they seem, then the human subject today is suffused with a certain groundlessness, what Milan Kundera might call the unbearable lightness of being. What's more, the human subject can only create the illusion of "substance" by cultivating his or her pain and, additionally, the power to inflict pain. This pain is the insignia of membership in the social machinery that has sufficient power to make its awful presence so pointedly felt and so darkly attractive. In short, pain signals that one is an "insider" in the community as chamber of horrors, the community as masochism cult.

How else can we explain why a student would report to his teacher on the first day of class that working on an essay is like chewing on a rock?

The opposite possibility, however, clearly persists, and, in the writing classroom, it seems to ghost along in the domain of prose style. As I noted in the last chapter, pleasure can serve as an index to the clarity of a text; it can signal a felt sense of connection to an audience; it can mean that, through careful, critical reflection on the word-by-word arrangement of one's sentences, one has created an opening, a conduit between self and other. What I've described here is not the cultivation of personal voice nor of disciplinary discourse, but something that, while perhaps bearing traces of both of these, is finally something else altogether: an immersion in fairly technical questions of prose style in order to exploit the transpersonal power of sound. To write this way means engaging one's language not as a static object, never a rock to chew on, but as a dynamic, temporal event, a sequence of moments. Precisely this latter sense of language would seem to suffuse our use of speech, at least unconsciously, as we strive for one sort of connection or another with a listener. Thus, the goal of my writing classroom is to help students to use this more or less intuitive, speech-based, verbal power as consciously and deliberately as possible when they write.

Of course, I can foster no such transformation simply through exercises. Rather, what I'm after is the sort of generative magic at the heart of speech by which words beget words, the generative magic manifest in inward dialogue and constructive self-criticism about what sequences of words, in a given situation, feel best. While I can't make this magic available through handbook exercises, I can respond to students' writing with as full an awareness as possible of what, exactly, this magic is and what, in its most powerful forms, it can do. To say it another way, I'm not simply interested in wordplay for its own sake. Rather, when writers work with style, they can open the way for a much deeper sort of pleasure: an increased sense of well-being, an increased sense of power in the social world. In short, the pleasure of crafting sentences and paragraphs, as I discovered recently, can blossom in students into in a grander phenomenon—that is, a therapeutic phenomenon.

When writing "heals," the writer is not simply erasing his or her pain, but transforming that pain into knowledge, into the renewed capacity for actively engaging the world, for building, entering, and influencing communities. Those most skeptical about the relevance of "logotherapy" to contemporary composition pedagogy might caricature this sort of writing as a mawkish immersion in memories of primal trauma, even a more or less neurotic, inward repetition of one's most numbing experiences. But I would like to describe logotherapy in this chapter in terms of an engagement with prose style, for I believe that, as a writer becomes more and more adept at organizing language, a corresponding confidence can grow, as well, in her reflections about her innermost experience and about the surrounding world. In other words, the sort of critical reflection about style I'm advocating can anchor and support increasingly ambitious personal reflection and social critique. Thus, we should not suppose that the sort of work with style I outlined in the last chapter is mere fun, mere play. On the contrary, such work is just what Gorgias and the other sophists claimed it is: powerful medicine. An immersion in style is a microcosm for what an education in rhetoric tries to achieve, for it can open the student to the possibility that becoming a better writer means, at least in part, learning how to use writing to become a healthier, stronger participant in the world.

I'm certainly not calling for teachers of writing to convert their courses into group therapy sessions. Nor am I suggesting that universities require a first-year course in the personal essay, nor even that the standard first-year course require more personal writing. Rather, I wish simply to dwell on certain possibilities in the tradition of rhetoric that bear directly on a familiar classroom situation. As Anderson and MacCurdy note in this chapter's second epigraph, no matter what we assign, some students will gravitate, inevitably and intuitively, toward a certain way of practicing writing, one that engages traumatic experience for purposes of taking power over and through those memories. To respond productively to those papers, as MacCurdy argues, we must carefully rethink the ways our classrooms have traditionally configured the relationships between teacher and student, text and author, public and private discourse, writing for "growth" and writing to heal. In short, we need to understand logotherapy.

Why Logotherapy?

As I noted in the first chapter, the suicide rate among teenagers has quadrupled in the last three decades (Derksen and Strasburger 1996, 67). As the first epigraph to this chapter notes, the students who appear in composition classrooms every fall on campuses across the country have just recently left behind a world where nearly one in three of them, at one time or another, wanted to die. And a good many of them want to hand in writing that, even when not required to do so, engages the domain of the intensely personal. Perhaps today's students are in danger of losing all contact with their doubles and are suffering their schooling as a grim process of modernization in which they gradually internalize an abstract ideal before which, as I noted in Chapter 1, they can only masochistically grovel. When this relationship fails—that is, when students weary of cultivating pain—then the deeper misery arises that we see reflected in the dreadful statistics. Perhaps they hand in those sorrowful essays as part of a larger, personal struggle to heal themselves. Perhaps, too, if we can teach them how to work with style, we can help them regain a pleasure-filled relation with their doubles, one that will clarify and sharpen the inward reflection and social critique that their experience supports, even demands.

Unfortunately, most students have already picked up innumerable cues that the writing they do in school cannot possibly serve as a tool for personal growth and empowerment; they certainly don't see this writing as a medium for the therapeutic pleasures of connecting to a larger community. They come into their writing courses, in fact, with just the opposite sense. Consider what Guy Allen reports on some surveys he has conducted at the beginning of a nonrequired course in writing that he has taught as many as five times a year over fifteen years:

- More than 85 percent report their dread of writing in an academic setting.
- More than 70 percent of incoming students report that they take the writing course to reduce the number of "mistakes" they make in their writing.
- More than 65 percent of students feel that they must keep themselves out of their writing.

These statistics suggest a significant degree of alienation. Indeed, in my own informal survey a few years ago, I asked students to define as carefully as they could the precise nature of any pleasure they had experienced while writing. The overwhelming answer: relief at having finished the task.

Most students, it seems, have been sutured into a certain kind of subject-position, a certain place in a larger mythology, in which the role of writing student seems to embed a powerful stigma. As far as authorial pleasure goes, many likely assume, quite simply, that you-can't-get-there-from-here and that writing in school essentially means chewing on a rock. These students seem keenly sensitized to the sort of social order that Susan Miller convincingly sketches in *Textual Carnivals* (1991): the academic community locates the student of writing at the lowest possible position in the discursive hierarchy of the English Department, many fathoms below teachers of writing, who are in turn far below the teachers of literature, who are themselves but the lowly servants of canonical literary icons like Shakespeare and Milton. Students undoubtedly encounter the academy, thus configured, not so much as a discursive democracy but rather as a place ruled by a brutalizing logic of insiders versus outsiders, "them" versus "us" (see Harris 1996, 100). And moving from outside to inside requires something like a mystical leap of mind, a sort of religious conversion (1996, 103). Many students perhaps come to imagine that such a conversion requires a renunciation of the "sinful ways" of their home culture, their own language and habits of mind (see Richard Rodriguez 1993). Within such a logic, the sorrowful statistics reported by Allen and by Berman and Schiff are rather less surprising.

Students, in fact, seem fully attuned to the point Richard Miller makes in a passage I footnoted toward the end of the first chapter: the academy does not particularly value writing that provides real benefits to the writer but only in writing that verifies the author's ability to serve the academy. Because most classrooms apparently do little to encourage the seriousness of the students' personal investment in their work, most students are quick to diminish any sense of personal connection. As Guy Allen puts it, when students first enter his classroom, they seem to have "no idea that writing could be a part of life. Life for them resumed after they got their essays in" (251). This wholly artificial split between the "personal" and the "academic," Allen argues, is at the heart of the so-called literacy crisis that cycles through the media at regular intervals and generates a great deal of hand-wringing at faculty meetings. Echoing the argument about "Engfish" that Ken Macrorie made nearly forty years ago, Allen suggests that "The 'writing problem' we hear so much about in the university is really a 'meaning problem.'" He explains, "Students learn to fake meaning . . . and [those] who honor this survival strategy with terms like 'bullshitting,' do not confuse it with making meaning. They feel sure it has no meaning" (280). This absence of meaning is, I can't help but believe, the presence of pain. In a remark that would seem related to the one about chewing on a rock, one of my students, Jason Vicari, responded to that final in-class essay prompt by proclaiming, in part, "I do not enjoy papers that I have to 'bullshit' (for lack of a better word) my way through. I think that there is nothing that bothers me more about writing than a paper full of BS."

Perhaps we can begin to account for Jason's acute displeasure at having to "bullshit" his way through an assignment and, in turn, virtually everyone's hunger for a more engaging experience with language and the world by falling back on a familiar argument, a variation of the one I sketched a moment ago with reference to the painful malaise of postmodern consumer culture. If contemporary society is characterized by the relatively widespread erosion of the meta-narratives that have traditionally structured our experience of historical time (the Christian myth of Christ's eventual return, the myth of scientific progress toward a techno-utopia, the myth of the eventual emancipation of all workers, and so on), then students are left to face the world without the kind of narrative context that allows them to dialogue about, make sense of, and thereby assuage the inevitable injuries that accompany the moment-to-moment stream of immediate, temporal experience. Naturally, they crave a chance to interpret, to make meaning out of their lives, for otherwise they must succumb to a feeling of powerlessness, a feeling of being "taken over by alien experiences [they] could not anticipate and did not choose," which, as Charles Anderson and Marian MacCurdy note, is the stuff of trauma (5). Indeed, this sort of experience, Anderson and MacCurdy assert, is a defining feature of the second half of the twentieth century, and they add, "even witnesses to disasters can be susceptible to the effects of PTSD [post-traumatic stress disorder]" (4).

While some may object to the idea that trauma is a pervasive, even a definitive feature of contemporary culture, such objections become increasingly difficult, Anderson and MacCurdy imply, when one considers certain distinctive trends of the last half-century: the proliferation of nuclear arms; the campaigns of genocide in Africa, Southeast Asia, and Eastern Europe; the horrendous bloodshed that has accompanied the rise of the post- or neo-colonial order; the "backlash" against women and minorities in the wake of the progress of the '60s and '70s; the plight of minority populations trapped in dying inner cities, while wealth is increasingly concentrated in the hands of an ever-shrinking segment of the population, one that seems bent on the piece-by-piece dismantling of the social safety net; the advent of new, deadly microorganisms like HIV, Ebola, and resistant strains of TB and pneumonia; the horrifying events of September 11th, 2001, the anthrax scare that followed, and the significant threat of more such events. Given all of these trends and the wider social fragmentation that inevitably accompanies them, given the ways merely witnessing such events can affect people, Anderson and MacCurdy argue, "PTSD has become a central, material" feature of our time (4).

If today's college students have come of age in a cultural moment of relatively widespread PTSD, then perhaps they can't help but seek, in their writing, a cure. Although we surely can't recreate those collapsed meta-narratives to shelter them against the trauma that the postmodern condition constantly precipitates, we can at least respond to their writing with an awareness of a miniature counter-narrative, one about certain possibilities that arise whenever people struggle to write, one that has been eloquently described every now and again by people interested in rhetoric since the pre-Classical era.

I offer an account of the tradition of logotherapy in this chapter not as an exhaustive, airtight history, but rather as patchwork of curious moments that help me make sense of my students' responses to that final in-class essay prompt. As my students' essays show, the possibility of writing as a kind of magical medicine is still very much alive among today's students at the level of intuition and the most grassroots sort of lore. Why then, shouldn't we keep such possibilities in mind as we teach, especially given the more or less pervasive misery of the postmodern student population?

Whether or not one accepts this premise of pervasive misery, we must agree that my colleague's student, who said that writing is like chewing on a rock, is by no means a rarity. Regrettably, all of us who have taught writing have seen a version of this student—usually in the back row, staring blankly at the floor, or off to one side, along the wall, hiding under a baseball cap or a curtain of long hair. While I hardly mean to suggest that those dour slackers who duck into our classes a few minutes late to roost languidly in the remote corners of the room face exactly the same struggles as those who have survived combat, rape, child abuse, or catastrophic accidents, I do think that we can apply what we've learned in recent years about trauma and recovery to that renegade tradition in the history of rhetoric that I've been describing, and, in turn, to the particular sorts of challenges we face in today's writing classroom.

That rock-chewing student, and, in fact, all of our toughest cases in the composition classroom can be described as having lost contact with their doubles, as having foreclosed their capacity for dialogue, as having become dumbstruck. These students can be thought of as mentally blocked or scattered by some memory that they can't articulate. And the work of reaching them, the work of making the power of rhetoric available to them, is very much akin to a healing process. To help them heal themselves, we need not push them to write about these painful memories, but rather we must only create for them the kind of rhetorical contexts that will allow them greater and greater access to the power of language. As they make this power their own, they will likely begin to apply it to their own lives in broader, more ambitious ways. That is, they can use it as a powerful tool against the debilitating effects of trauma.

As Judith Herman (1992) explains, when human subjects are threatened, they release significant reserves of adrenaline to energize themselves for fighting or fleeing, and, when neither option seems realistic, the memories of this awful moment are "not encoded like the ordinary memories of adults in a verbal, linear narrative that is [in turn] assimilated into an ongoing life story" (37); rather, Herman writes, such memories are encoded "in the form of vivid sensations and images" (38), which can spontaneously intrude as nightmares, morbid waking reveries and obsessions, or even hallucinations (41). The traumatic memory becomes an *idée fixe* that paralyzes and alienates the subject, like a rock to chew on, catching the subject's sense of time in a stranglehold that refuses to let him or her move forward or to interact happily with others. These symptoms, however, can diminish, and the subject can return to the rhythms of ongoing social experience, but only when such memories are rewoven into an ongoing narrative. Put simply, one can go some distance toward taming these memories when one writes about them; and, as writing heals the writer, time resumes, and the writer returns to the world (see Herman [1992], Chap. 9).

Of course, I would seem to beg a question here: just because a student has a hard time articulating *anything*, why must that mean that there is a deep, dark, *something* concealed beneath—and causing—their botched, abortive attempts at writing? How can I claim that traumatic memories cause all problems with writing? I certainly don't think that they do. Rather, I'd like to set aside this simplistic, causal logic to suggest that trauma and writing troubles are much more complicatedly inter-twined. That is, while trauma can cause writing troubles, writing troubles can begin to affect students traumatically, for, as they develop writer's block or become too overwhelmed by the pressures of college to produce clear, readable prose, students can feel that in flunking out they are forfeiting the most important opportunity for advancement they will ever have, that they are "falling off the conveyor belt . . . onto the filth-strewn floor." Obviously, such an experience is traumatic. And so, trauma and writing troubles are sufficiently intertwined that we can suppose that when we help students with their writing we are providing them with powerful tools for countering trauma.

However, because traumatic experience can never be *completely* subsumed in a smooth narrative of normal temporal sequencing, it be-comes, says Slavoj Zizek (2002), something akin to a point of "eternity" against which the ongoing stream of time defines itself. "If trauma were to be successfully temporalized/historicized," writes Zizek, "the very dimension of time would implode/collapse into an eternal, timeless Now" (96), and this euphoric apocalypse would be the perfect mirror-reverse of the traumatic moment. The tension between this possibility and the traumatic memory itself drives the experience of time, and the process of healing is the ongoing struggle to push toward that happier possibility, that reversal of trauma, the apocalyptic redemption.

Back to the intricate intertwining of writing troubles and trauma: we are all committed to this struggle, for when we first begin to speak and to respond to the utterances of others, we are, as in trauma, taken over by an alien experience we did not anticipate or choose; we are suddenly exposed to the power of sound in a completely new way, engulfed in an exchange of meanings that we can never fully compre-hend or control, a most pointed version of the power of sound to over-ride the individual will. In short, the moment we enter language, we suffer a blow, a wound, and we will forever after try to use language to recover from this blow. This moment is known, in the language of psychoanalysis, as symbolic castration, and, in the next chapter, I'll say more about how it ushers us into language and gives rise to the ego. For now, suffice to say that in this broad, abstract sense, we all suffer from—and strive to overcome—a traumatic memory that initiates us into worldly subjectivity. The founding trauma of each individual's existence is made to reverberate by traumatic incidents and is perhaps even amplified by them, creating a yet more dire need in human subjects to heal themselves from that initial, mind-boggling plunge into the verbal tensions between self and other.

When the struggle to reverse primal trauma is going well, our prose is less likely to seem a fragmentary, vague, repetitive chaos; when it isn't, our writing suffers from precisely these disconnections. As teachers, we can lay the groundwork for positive transformation by helping students become comfortable with strategies for writing more clearly, more effectively. Specifically, the immersion in style that I recommend can open the way for the transformation of pain into knowledge and power, the reentry of the alienated sufferer back into the community; it can restore doubles and actualize the renegade idea that selves, texts, and worlds are dynamic, interanimating processes; it can give pleasure. In its profoundest form, it can heal.

In fact, this is exactly the way the domain of style has been understood by a long tradition of rhetorical healers. What's more, these ideas, though rarely engaged by the field of composition, continue to circulate within our culture, for the kinds of dramatic transformations my students describe not only hinge on an immersion in style but are also understood by my students, in their relatively off-the-cuff remarks, in ways that directly echo thinkers who are quite remote from the scene of contemporary writing instruction. In fact, in their responses to that last essay assignment, in which I asked them to explain what makes writing fun, all seventeen of my students suggested that a crucial element in pleasurable writing is knowing how to engage the domain of style. And, what's more, a good many of them understood this pleasure not as mere "fun," but as a very serious thing—an experience essential to their humanity, and, as I'll argue here, one with a long, complex history.

Plato's Medical Philosophy Versus the Writer's Cathartic Self-Invention

As I noted in Chapter 1, those who treated disease in the centuries immediately preceding the classical era began to take a greater and greater interest in what Pedro Lain Entralgo calls its *primitive* character (1970, 39–40). "Disease, the punishment of a personal fault, of a collective transgression, or of a crime of one's ancestors, was popularly conceived," as

Entralgo puts it, "as the contamination of the individual 'nature' of the patient by a more or less invisible *miasma* or by a god or a demon" (40–41). Disease marked one's moral character, one's ethos or personality—and it signified the presence of some other entity, some other ethos, a god or demon come to punish the sufferer. As this belief intensified in the years leading to Plato, new categories of disease emerged, and various magical, cathartic, verbal therapies became more and more frequent. Specifically, healers used verbal charms, prayers, and incantations to drive out the invading, punishing entity and to restore the patient's public identity to one of moral purity (Entralgo 1970, xvii).

Of course, this healing language was not generated by the sufferer but by the physician, a fact that would seem to undermine any analogy to today's practice of therapeutic writing. The process of healing, however, hinges—then as now—precisely on overcoming the boundaries that divide author and audience. And thus the fact that, in classical antiquity, the verbal healer and the sufferer were not the same person does not undercut the analogy to today's practice of writing as healing, but instead gives us clues as to how, exactly, this latter practice might work. Specifically, the healing chants, incantations, and prayers of the ancients constitute a kind of carefully stylized language that serves as a bridge between self and other, a conduit by which the stigmatized sufferer is cathartically released back into the community.

Perhaps this process is what my student, Jason Vicari, meant when he responded to that last assignment about what makes writing fun by asserting, "I believe writing is fun because it allows me to emphasize and express my opinions when I am sometimes too shy or quiet to say it out loud." Jason continues, "Writing changes that in a way that I have no one to interrupt me and my fear of being rejected fades away." In fact, when Jason reports that "I know that when I write, I prove my opinion in a way that will not be easily rejected," he is referring presumably to a way that relies on carefully disciplined style: when he writes, he not only knows how to "express" his opinion but how to "emphasize" and "prove" his opinion. And because his opinion cannot "be easily rejected," he is using his understanding of style to reverse his feelings of alienation. In this sense, style has for Jason the same sort of power that the ancients understood it to have: a therapeutic power.

For example, one of the ancient practitioners of verbal healing, Antiphon, understood himself to be playing upon the dynamics between *nomos* and *physis*. In the simplest terms, Antiphon manipulated the dynamics between discourse and the body. More specifically, *nomos* means law, an established convention or way of being, an ethos, or a discursive position, precisely the sort of thing associated with distinctively stylized language. And *physis* refers to the natural, spontaneous, material experience of the human body. For Antiphon, negotiating this tension between *nomos* and *physis* with words was the essence of all rhetorical practice. Indeed, Antiphon believed that "By means of the persuasion of the rhetorician, the patient, painfully and helplessly situated within his own *nomos* and unable to escape from it alone, succeeds in placing himself in another" (Entralgo 1970, 101). In other words, Antiphon knew that if his culture understood illness as the mark of moral impurity, of a punishing invader, then illness was a signifier that could be altered by a steady stream of different sorts of signifiers—sacred songs and chants. Antiphon's words/spirits could expunge the other signifier or, by wrapping it in a new verbal context, change its meaning, inducing a purifying, cathartic transformation of the sufferer.

Consider the way one of my students describes the personal transformation that his engagement with prose style enabled. In response to that prompt about what makes writing fun, Josh Peysach wrote, in part:

> Fun? Writing fun? To use these two words in the same sentence would have been unheard of last year. I doubted my writing skills and techniques, even though I didn't use any. But lately, I began to realize what it is I was trying to say, or write, in my essays . . .
>
> And when something comes easy to us, we can really start to find it fun . . .
>
> After writing started to become easier and easier, I found myself getting more and more into everything I was writing. I started to think about what needed to be said instead of just writing BS. Instead of BS, I put down my thoughts and feelings that were formerly just bottled inside my head. This year I began to use writing as an outlet, instead of using it to get a grade in class. When I'm not writing, lately I've been thinking of writing my thoughts down and in what ways to write them down.

For Josh, style has transformed his sense of himself as a writer, and, what's more, his new sense of technical prowess has provided him with the tools to undertake further, more personal transformation. Another student this semester, Amber Brook, says that writing allows her much the same power I described a moment ago in connection with Antiphon. Here is part of her response to that essay topic:

> My writing allows me to be myself or to completely reinvent myself. I can be myself in my diary. I can be someone else when I write a letter to an old friend. I can be another completely different person when I write a letter to my boss or to a co-worker. My writing allows me to lie or to tell the truth. I can make it happy, sad, scary, funny, honest, or dishonest. I can make the world seem like a better place by using my imagination and writing down my thoughts.

Amber feels that, through writing, she can open an array of options for her public personae, casting off and reinventing these selves at will in order to connect with her audience, much the way Antiphon's practice of verbal medicine could.

Admittedly, exactly how the experience my students describe could, in ancient times, literally cure disease is difficult for today's mind to fathom, but surely the ancient experience of reuniting with the community, of overcoming alienation and stigma, must have carried with it a powerful, physical sense of release, a cathartic feeling of liberation that provides a useful template for understanding later practices of writing as healing, as well as the way today's students experience the growth of their rhetorical abilities.

Both Josh and Amber describe writing in terms of freedom. Josh says that "When I can better communicate myself . . . I find that it gives me a profound sense of freedom that nothing else can give me." And Amber says, "I love to write for many reasons. The biggest reason would be freedom of expression." This freedom, however, is explicitly anchored in particular commitments. As Josh puts it, "I found myself getting more and more into everything I was writing . . . instead of just writing BS." And Amber's sense of open-ended self-invention is contingent on the audience she wants to reach. Presumably, when students don't feel this freedom or any impulse to connect with their texts or their audiences, they write only so much "BS." This BS, as Guy Allen suggests, has the peculiar capacity to thrive in school settings and, as Jason implies, has a primary relationship to student displeasure.

I can't help but suspect that the unpleasant experience of school-based writing for these students is the long-term legacy of the sharp criticism that the classical era aimed at Antiphon and the other rhetorical healers. Perhaps because this older medicine was driven underground, our students today tap into residual traces of it with a feeling of having made an exhilarating discovery, one that, they intuitively sense, runs counter to the overwhelming weight of the mainstream Western tradition of the last two and a half millennia. For, thanks in large measure to Plato's attack on these sophistic therapists in the fifth century B.C.E., a different, more "scientific" medicine emerged—one that emphasized not words but diet, drugs, and surgery (Entralgo 1970, xviii); and that, as such, spearheaded a powerful attack on rhetoric as the domain of sheer "BS" that, of course, persists today. In fact, this new, antirhetorical medicine was identified tellingly by Virgil as the "mute art" (xviii), and, though the newer "silent" physicians of Greece were charged by a character in Plato's *Charmides* with an insufficient grasp of the way the ailments of the body can stem from the soul or from the emotions (xviii), this "mute art" gradually replaced the older verbal medicine.

Plato began his attack on rhetoric by creating a taxonomy of the arts, and this taxonomy was organized around a fundamental division between the arts of the soul and those of the body. The principle art of the soul is philosophy, and its counterparts in the body are medicine and gymnastic. Both of these bodily counterparts are distinguished, in turn, from a bogus version: the "counterfeit" of medicine is cooking, which aims at producing only pleasure rather than actual nourishment; and the counterfeit of gymnastic is cosmetics, which aims only at prettifying the body rather than actually strenthening it. Among these spurious, counterfeit arts, Plato located rhetoric: it traffics in mere illusions rather than the truths of spiritual well-being, and it seeks only to manipulate the body's senses, passions, and desires. Where philosophy is concerned with reason, truth, and goodness, rhetoric is concerned with mere style, appearance, and pleasure. Philosophy is to rhetoric as surgery is to petty dope peddling (see De Romilly 1992, 480–89). If that's all rhetoric is, then it is clear why no one wants to engage it with any depth: it *has no depth*. At best, it fleetingly manipulates the desires, senses, and passions of the body; at worst, it actively obscures the timeless truths of the soul.

The notion that writing has little value would seem to have shaped, until just recently, the education of at least one of my students. Here is a passage from Brad Monnet's response to that last in-class essay prompt:

> Writing is often viewed by many as a punishment. I can remember growing up, teachers and instructors would give "busy" work. . . . These images of what writing is still dwell in my mind. The images of writing as something I hate to do has always been part of me until recently. Recently, I have learned to enjoy my writings. I enjoy expressing my thoughts in written words.
>
> When we write out our thoughts it gives us time to see what is really going on in our minds. It gives us a chance to evaluate the important things on our mind. Sometimes when you write out your thoughts it's easier to deal with them. Also while writing out my thoughts I have learned to communicate my feelings better to others. Feelings sound better when written out first then presented to someone. Your words are more in order when you write them, therefore you sound better and more confident when you speak your feelings.
>
> Sounding a lot better and being more confident in my writings had to come from the usage of stylistic devices.

Obviously, these stylistic devices are, as I claimed, powerful medicine, and Plato's attack on those who developed them and built educational curricula around them would seem to warrant closer scrutiny. Indeed, as Jasper Neel (1988) has taught us, we can't quite trust Plato, nor, as my students might add, should we trust institutions that define writing as, at best, a punishing brand of busywork. After all, while Plato repeatedly attacks writing and rhetoric in his "Seventh Letter" and in *The Phaedrus*, he does this, of course, *in writing and with extraordinary rhetorical skill*. He uses a powerful tool to criticize that same tool so that no one else will take an interest in it, much less start using it to develop ideas and arguments to rival Plato's (Neel 1988, 6). In fact, Plato is himself, argues Neel, all of the things he condemns—a skilled writer, a rhetor, a sophist—and Plato identified his work by a different name, scapegoating his actual methods, because he wanted to steer people away from these methods and thereby significantly diminish the power of others to rival him.

Are students like Josh, Jason, Brad, and, for that matter, countless others the victims of Plato's trick? Have they been taught to dread writing as meaningless busywork, what they call so much "BS," and to look elsewhere for the spectacular sorts of powers that writing makes available? If so, then perhaps we can suggest that when my students engaged in the pleasures of style they tapped into residual traces of a far less famous school of philosophers, a group that immediately followed the classical era and that was rather less circumspect than Plato about its methods. These were the Hellenistic philosophers—the Epicureans, the Skeptics, and the Stoics—and they explicitly embraced writing and rhetoric as primary tools in fulfilling their most important task. Though I have no evidence that my students have ever heard of this philosophic tradition, it would seem to imbue, as we'll see, their thinking about their writing, through and through.

The Hellenistic philosophers understood their task, Martha Nussbaum explains, as therapy. They devoted themselves to "addressing the most painful problems of human life" (Nussbaum 1994, 3). They understood the philospher, Nussbaum adds, "as a compassionate physician whose arts could heal many pervasive types of human suffering." Moreover, these philosopher/healers were not simply interested in the inner lives of their patients, but in the ways these inner lives were constructed, supported, and, most important, deformed by powerful social forces (11). In other words, because they saw pain as a pervasive feature of human experience, they refused to think of their work in terms of "detached displays of cleverness" (11). Rather, what enables philosophy to perform the important work of healing individuals and, at the same time, criticizing society is philosophy's commitment to "precise reasoning, logical rigor, and definitional precision" (15).

These philosophers understood that none of these commitments would be possible without writing. What's more, these philosophers believed deeply in rhetoric: "[A] precise, logically rigorous argument that is not well-suited to the needs of its hearers, an argument that is simply and entirely academic and unable to engage its listeners in a practical way," is, for these thinkers, "a *defective philosophical argument*" (15). If Philosophy is to perform its primary function—its medical function—it must be wholly intertwined with "complex arts of speech and writing" (16). The essential focus of the Stoic's therapeutic discourse, in particular, is the careful, watchful, ongoing criticism of appearances (327). Therapy, in this sense, means cultivating critical skill, the ability to spot mistaken or problematic trends in behavior and thought, and this capacity for critique must ultimately take the form of a shrewd sense of verbal style. As Nussbaum puts it, the "rhetorical and literary dimensions of an argument are not mere incidental frills," (330); they are at the core of what Stoics would study. Thus, the Stoic project would seek to collapse Plato's essential premise—his primary distinction between philosophy and rhetoric, between the truths of the soul and the desires of the body.

Stoics not only study verbal devices, they also use them. Their discourse is always rooted in concrete examples and narratives and is rife with verbal figures and tropes (338). In fact, Stoics believed that the educational curriculum should foreground literary texts as tools that enhance self-reflection, promote social criticism, and, perhaps above all, demonstrate powerful verbal techniques (351). One of the most important of the Stoics—Chrysippus—wrote a four-volume treatise that climaxed with a book that was sometimes called the *therapeutikon* and other times known as the *ethikon,* for it was a book about healing, how to feel happy, and, as such, a book about ethics, the proper conduct of life. Interestingly enough, Chrysippus was passionately interested in writing, filling his work with "scores of observations on ordinary usage, on common expressions, on literary passages" (368–69). A commitment to this critical power (and its concrete manifestation in stylistic practice) is the root of a joyful life (398–401). And this joy is supremely social, for the critical, cathartic purging of false beliefs proceeds not solely within the individual but through the individual, the writer, in therapeutic service to the wider community that would otherwise perpetuate the damaging falsehoods.

Again, while some may suppose that all of this would seem quite remote from the immediate, practical realities of the first-year composition course, consider the way one of my students, Katrine Nordstrom, seems to have inherited, somehow, the same commitment that the Stoics advocated. In response to that last in-class essay assignment, she wrote:

> To be able to enjoy writing, you have to know what writing can do for you. With writing, you can attack, question, or even punch the reader in the face with what you have to say. You can manipulate your words to emphasize your arguments. You can use different writing methods in order to convey what you have to say. You can get the readers' sympathy, arouse their emotions, or make their stomach turn, all after how you choose to write. Best of all, you can play on, or with, the readers' emotions in a way that will benefit your cause.

Katrine clearly showcases a keen awareness of the powers of words to create—and to question—appearances, and she implicitly suggests that, because pleasurable writing is also writing that "will benefit your cause," she sees this writing as having a rich potential for social criticism. Even though I have no evidence that she has explicitly heard of the Stoics, it seems obvious that Katrine could be called one.

Where did Katrine get these ideas? If Stoic concepts of the power of style can be traced back to the sophists and even the pre-Socratic rhapsodes, they probably filtered their way through history to Katrine, at least in part, via the work of Longinus, in whom they find rich elaboration. Though written in the first centuries of the Christian era, as Thomas Benson tells us, there is no mention of Longinus' work by writers of his time; instead, his work only became widely known after an edition was printed in Basel in 1554. Nonetheless, it began to exert a powerful influence on European thought throughout the eighteenth century (1996 415), ultimately serving as a rallying point through that century for what George Kennedy (1999) calls a "cult of the sublime" (134). And, at the risk of getting ahead of myself, this "cult" played an important part in the development of Romanticism, which in turn powerfully influenced much of the popular lore about logotherapy that exists today.

For Longinus, the sublime is a feeling of "joy and vaunting" (80), a kind of cathartic transformation, and it can be made to erupt through stylistic devices. He devotes the bulk of his treatise, "On the Sublime," (1971) to defining and illustrating various verbal techniques, such as inversions, accumulations, variations, climaxes, periphrasis, and metaphor, similar to those I list in the appendix. The cathartic pleasures of style, however, are not wholly private, for Longinus insists, in the first paragraph of "On the Sublime," that he is writing his essay in the hopes that it will be "of use to the public man" (77). In other words, Longinus seeks an audience that is itself quite concerned with wielding power over and through an audience. Moreover, in this same opening paragraph, Longinus insists that the strong rhetor doesn't seek merely to persuade his audience, but to reach them in ways far more powerful and complete: "The effect of elevated speech upon an audience is not persuasion but transport. At every turn and in every way imposing speech, with the spell it throws over us, prevails over that which aims at [mere] persuasion and gratification" (77). In other words, Longinus' ideas about the sublime, and, implicitly, his sense of therapy, is that it shows the "public man" the way to greater and greater public power—not merely how to persuade an audience, but how to "transport" it. As such, he is supremely interested in the experience of connecting with the collective. This, I think, is what he means by the feeling of "joy and vaunting" that he calls "the sublime." It is the ultimate reversal of alienation and, as such, a kind of cure.

Though the idea may seem far-fetched, I think a number of my students had, by the end of a semester of working with style, begun to speak and write about their experience of composing in turns of thought that belong to this tradition. They had, in a sense, joined this Stoic "cult of the sublime." Consider again Josh's claim, the way it would seem to bear traces of Longinus' remarks about the sublime: "When I can better communicate myself . . . I find that it gives me a profound sense of freedom that nothing else can give me." And when Amber catalogues the variety of roles that writing allows her to invent for herself and suggests that the choices she makes about these roles are contingent on the particular audience for whom she is performing, she implies that this contingency in no way compromises her primary motivation for writing: "I love to write for many reasons. The biggest reason would be freedom of expression."

In other words, both Josh and Amber ultimately prize a freedom that is wholly bound to communication, to community, to context, and to style and structure. These values are, I can't help but believe, a legacy of Longinus' ideas about the sublime. As Longinus puts it, the empowerment of the "public man" depends, paradoxically, upon a certain self-dissolution: passages of sublimity must pour forth in a way "almost outstripping the speaker" (87). When not dissolved somehow by the power of the utterance, the rhetor can and must become dissolved in another way, for Longinus points to "the further case in which the writer, when relating something about a person, suddenly breaks off and converts himself into that selfsame person" (92). Obviously, for the sublime to erupt, it must erupt in a way that dissolves the author. That is, for the sublime to erupt, distinctions between authors and their subjects and between authors and their audiences must disappear.

When this happens, one feels flooded with extraordinary rhetorical power, a robust social vitality of the kind Amber, Josh, Brad, Jason, and Katrine describe. Most important, this feeling is not restricted to the author: it spreads contagiously through the audience, an experience of collective harmony in which the author is just one more humming particle. At the risk of over-simplification, Longinus might say that there is no such thing as one-person-experiencing-the-sublime or becoming healed, for these cathartic pleasures are by definition an affair of the multiple. They build and initiate one into community. As Katrine put it, "They can benefit your cause."

Recalling the rhapsodes and the sophists, Longinus describes the way music uses rhythm and harmony to hypnotize an audience into a grand, collective dance of solidarity, and then he argues that this is the essential purpose of written discourse as well: it must duplicate the harmonies and rhythms that, in organizing sound into music, organize the audience into a single, unified entity. In other words, the sublime does not simply reside within a well-composed text, but rather flashes through the text the way that sound fills an amphitheater, repeating itself in the audience, leading the audience to see itself as something like a unified composition, a consensus. The sublime text is a "harmonious structure" and it disposes us to "every emotion which it contains within itself." And the audience harkens not just to hear the harmony of the text, but to hear itself, through the text, as a single harmonious entity, "for [the composition] calls forth manifold shapes of words, thoughts, deeds, beauty, melody, all of them born at our birth and grown with our growth" (98).

If these "manifold shapes" are "all of them born at our birth and grown with our growth," they are coterminous with the audience's sense of itself, even at the level of physical being. Curiously enough, these mysterious "shapes" seem to embody or organize the transpersonal power of sound and thus they must be akin to the verbal figures, schemes, and tropes associated with the rhapsodes and sophists. They echo not only the earliest stages of the development of Western culture, but, curiously enough, early stages of childhood development, when the infant first begins to generate and use fundamental templates or schema to structure the experience of physical space and, in turn, to provide the basis for language acquisition.[1]

Thus the therapeutic pleasures that ensue as one gains more and more command over one's sentences and paragraphs can sometimes feel like what the religious call becoming "born again." Consider for example the essay that my student Tharon McDowell generated in response to that final in-class assignment. In order to unpack the full magnitude of what he claims about prose style and what it does for him, I'll have to quote Tharon's paper in full. Here it is:

Writing, The Creator of the Pen and I

Writing has been a tool I generally didn't use to express myself. I always opted to talk about what I'm feeling, or thinking through my mouth. It seemed easier, I guess. After using focus and flow, emphasis, and the stylistic devices, writing became enjoyable. Speaking on paper seems to be the word for it, writing that is. Now my thoughts are not only orated but also inscribed on a blank piece of paper. What a world I was not using. What a world I was hiding from. What a world I was dreading. My friend, the pen and I, are now as one.

For years, at least twenty, I hated English. Never wanting to write, or learn to write. I avoided at all cost writing papers, enlisting the help of a female to do it for me. It often worked due to my status as an athlete. Now I'm not, so the past is coming back to haunt me, and that is also why I dipped and dodged writing. You see my background has been one of a science and math nature. I thought writing an essay was a waste of time. Numbers and data need no verb, noun, adjective, or preposition. They did not feel binded by focus and flow, useless information in the eyes of a mathematician or a scientist. Man was I wrong about this!

I really didn't know how much was involved in the learning process. How all this is related to writing. Writing has procedures like math such as grammar. Writing has results such as emphasis. Writing has formulas such as focus and flow. Like math and its relationship to signs, writing has them too and they are called stylistic devices. There you have it, writing in the eyes of a science-natured person. Now it has been transformed from something I disliked into a necessary tool of expression.

After the past three months, this necessary tool of expression has offered me new ways to think and comprehend what I read. I read with a better understanding of what is being said in the essays. I notice the different tones being used. I also recognize probably the most joyable part of writing, the stylistic devices.

Stylistic devices are great tools of writing, [and] that makes creating and using them fun. You can live or die, mix and match, rearrange and change them to fit your every need. This can get pretty ugly, but if used wisely they can be implemented with the greatest of ease. Dam! I used one just talking about them (oxymoron). After all is said and done, the usage of these devices and others has made me rethink my view of writing.

At least once a week I write now, and I have noticed the improvement in my speech and grammar. That is what I must hail the most about writing. It has made me seem smarter, my conversation skills have soared, and my writing skills have surpassed my expectation. Who knows where this might lead. I might become a writer, you never know these days. But for the time being, I'm going to stick to the small things like being consistent, and adhering to principles of writing.

I thank this class for opening my mind and giving me the inspiration to write. I'm not hiding, running, skating, or passing writing off anymore. The pen became a friend, the paper is our lover, and writing is our creator. We all will be joined until we expire, but until then let the courtship live on.

Clearly, Tharon's account of his experience of writing dramatically contrasts with that of the student who said that writing was like chewing on a rock. Indeed, Tharon describes a sort of three-way marriage between self, pen, and paper, as if pen and paper had become his doubles and adds, "We will all be joined until we expire." Tharon describes his previous experience of writing as a waste of time, and says that writing, for him, was a world that he hid from, dreaded, and hated. Now, however, it has become a "necessary tool," one that he apparently takes up "at least once a week," one that, indeed, he must "hail" as "our creator." Again, Tharon's transformation seems tantamount to a religious awakening.

I am particularly intrigued by Tharon's repeated references to time: in the first two paragraphs, he describes a twenty-year stretch when he actively avoided writing; in the fourth paragraph, he describes the way the three months of the past semester have changed his concept of writing; in the sixth paragraph, he describes the present in terms of regular, weekly intervals in which he notices his rhetorical skill continuing to grow and wonders with palpable excitement about where, in the future, this might lead. And he ends this paragraph with a resolute, disciplined focus on the present ("For the time being, I'm going to stick to the small things like being consistent, and adhering to principles of writing") and a commitment to making sure his current absorption in the present persists ("let the courtship live on"). I think Tharon refers so often to matters of time and ends his essay with that resolute, even erotic absorption in the present, precisely because his new-found skills as a writer have begun to open for him the possibility of what bell hooks would call "the infinite" or what, earlier in this chapter, I called eternity—that mirror-reverse of trauma that is the very essence of the magical, the therapeutic, the sublime, the ecstatic.

As I noted at the outset of the chapter, trauma is a pervasive, even defining feature of our time, and given that everyone's entry into language, into the swirl of meanings that forever override the individual will, proceeds in ways broadly analogous to trauma, we can surely think about students' difficulties with writing not simply as a symptom or a source of trauma, but as a stressful, rock-chewing experience of alienation that, in fact, *repeats* primal trauma. What the Stoic tradition describes and what my students seem to have figured out is that learning to play with style can give them a kind of erotic relation to the Otherness of language, rather than a traumatic, alienating one; that such an approach to writing can precipitate a reversal of primal trauma and its constant repetition in postmodern culture; it can give them a new sense of the moment-to-moment stream of time and, in turn, of their own personal history, one in which the experience of eternity can flower.

Where trauma, as we noted in the last chapter, is the feeling of being taken over by an alien experience that one did not anticipate or choose, that one cannot interpret or connect to an ongoing sense of one's life story, the opposite sort of experience—an experience of eternity or infinity—appears with equal abruptness to provide one with supportive, even propulsive strength within the flowing world of time. Eternity, as Slavoj Zizek explains, "is not atemporal in the simple sense of persisting 'beyond' time; it is rather [that which] sustains, opens up, the dimension of temporality . . ." Eternity and Time are thus far from being opposed; rather, as William Blake says in *The Marriage of Heaven and Hell*, "Eternity is in love with the Productions of Time." In other words, each exists only in a dynamic with the opposite dimension, only through the mediation of the other.

I want to linger a little longer over Tharon's paper. I also want to offer a little more historical background and a few more conceptual tools that teachers might bear in mind as they interact with students, moment by moment, in the writing classroom. With this broad understanding of Tharon's paper, this wider historical context, and these more recent conceptual tools in mind, teachers will have more and more resources with which to help students compose pleasure.

Note

1. See Jean Mandler's 1991 work on the cognitive development of infants ("Conceptual Primitives"), as well as Mark Johnson's book, *The Body in the Mind* (1987), and Hildy Miller's article "Sites of Inspiration: Where Writing Is Embodied in Image and Emotion" in *Presence of Mind: Writing and the Domain Beyond the Cognitive* (1994).

Four

Desire and the Question of What the Teacher Does

I must mention it because it's so exceedingly important, so rich in hopes for the future, perhaps the most important of all the activities of analysis. What I am thinking of is the application of psycho-analysis to education.

—Sigmund Freud,
New Introductory Lectures,
1933

But first the notion that man has a body distinct from his soul is to be expunged; this I shall do by printing in the infernal method, by corrosives, which in hell are salutary and medicinal, melting apparent surfaces away and displaying the infinite which was hid.
—William Blake,
*The Marriage of Heaven
and Hell*

Tharon's paper far exceeds the ideas in my superficial sketch of the renegade tradition. Nonetheless, while I would hardly hope to prove chains of cause and effect that connect earlier and later figures in this tradition, much less suggest that each successive edition of these ideas embodies, identically, some universal truth that Tharon has articulated for us yet again, I find myself continuing to wonder about Tharon's paper, about how the renegade tradition reaches from antiquity into the contemporary classroom, and about what aspects of my teaching might have laid the groundwork for the transformation he describes. How the pre-Socratic rhapsodes may have made possible the sophists and how, in turn, a medical aspect of sophistry may have led to the Stoics and Longinus, does not, after all, tell me as much as I'd like to know about how Tharon could come to say that "The pen became a friend, the paper is our lover, and writing is our creator. We all will be joined until we expire, but until then let the courtship live on." However, by setting Tharon's paper alongside more recent renditions of the renegade and reflecting carefully on how I imagine my own role as a teacher, I can perhaps eventually understand Tharon's experience well enough to imagine ways to make versions of it increasingly available to more of my students.

As I mentioned in connection with the excerpt from Katrine's paper, Longinus' work became in the eighteenth century a rallying point for a certain "cult of the sublime" that, in turn, set the stage for English Romanticism. And Romanticism came to influence much of the popular lore about the psychotherapeutic powers of writing currently circulating in today's culture. More specifically, the version of Romanticism expounded in the 1950s in M. H. Abrams' highly influential book, *The Mirror and the Lamp* (1953), partnered with a closely related and widely popular body of work on the value of what was called "self-actualization" in the same decade to yield the expressivist approach to writing instruction that marked our field in the 1960s and 1970s (Berlin 1987, 146–47). And so, I wonder if Tharon—a nontraditional or "returning" student in his mid-30s—perhaps took classes some twenty-odd years ago, as I did, that were imbued with this Romantic-therapeutic or expressivist line of thought, and whether such classes could have engendered the potential for his experience in my class.

Nothing in Tharon's paper, however, echoes the central concerns usually attributed to expressivism; he nowhere talks about discovering his true voice or liberating some "inner me" from oppressive institutional conventions. On the contrary, he describes primarily a change of attitude toward writing that is rooted in his discovery of certain stylistic principles and devices that make his writing more readable, more engaging. And, rather than describing this change purely in terms of self-expression, the metaphors he uses are profoundly social. He says that the immersion in style has brought him a new lover (the paper) that he shares with his friend (the pen), and he sees writing now in terms of a "courtship" and as a "world." These are not at all the standard tropes usually attributed to the Romantic-therapeutic or expressivist approach to writing instruction. Nonetheless, I do think this tradition is worth reconsidering as a key source of ideas on authorial pleasure, ideas that perhaps we need only upgrade to make them useful in the thinking about Tharon's paper and the papers of all our students.

Many Romantics, particularly Rousseau, Wordsworth, and Co-
leridge, understood education, in a significant departure from the mainstream of their day, as a process of cultivating the students' intrinsic
qualities. Rather than assume, as most of their contemporaries did, that
children were suffused with original sin, that, if left alone, children
would turn to crime, and that education should therefore impose from
a position far removed from the child's life-world a redeeming but often
brutal baptism in factual knowledge, the Romantics conversely insisted
that children must be encouraged to cultivate—through experience,
reflection, perception, and, of course, immersion in the realm of the
"natural"—their intrinsic capacity for imagination. Such an approach
could assuage the alienating effects and emotional injuries of the opposite curriculum, the one meant to redeem them from original sin, and it
could also better prepare students for meaningful participation in the
community and in the life of the nation.[1] Much the same emphasis
appears in Matthew Arnold's thinking when he insisted that education
must stimulate the imagination by focusing on the pleasures of poetic
language. This line of thought perhaps extends into the twentieth
century through John Dewey's work, especially in his emphasis on the
imagination as "the large and generous blending of interests" that "ani-
mates and pervades all processes of making and observation" (quoted in
Gradin 1995, 45), an imagination we can cultivate, as I noted in Chapter 2, when we encourage students to play with language.

This interest in art, play, and imagination figured heavily in a series
of articles in the latter half of the 1960s on how writing teachers could
usefully set up their classrooms along the same lines that avant-garde
artists envisioned "The Happening," a possibility that Geoffrey Sirc has
recently urged us to revive in a book full of today's theoretical
sophistication that he named after an article from that period, *English
Composition as a Happening* (2002). Analogously, I can't help but wonder
about how Romantic concepts of the imagination can be translated
into or revived by contemporary ideas about desire. After all, the way
that Romantics cast the imagination and the ways that psychoanalytic
theorists cast desire are quite similar: both are intrinsic, pervasive, social, highly pleasurable integrations of work and play that are virtually
all-powerful in shaping perception and spurred along by the results of
their own activity. In fact, just as the teacher influenced by Romanticism would work toward cultivating the student's imagination, the
teacher influenced by psychoanalysis, analogously, would guide the
student, as Mark Bracher puts it, in "assuming unconscious desire"(1999, 2).

When a student learns to "assume unconscious desire," he or she
learns to acknowledge, appreciate, even rely upon the fact that to look
at some object—say, an emerging text—with detached neutrality,

stripped of desire, is to see, in the midst of such futility, at best a hazy blot, at least compared to how the object appears when looked at it in the opposite way. If the student learns to set aside a particular structure of resistance (called the ego, about which I'll say more shortly) and allow his or her sensory experience to be permeated with desire—corrupted, colored, and distorted by desire—then he or she will see the object much more vividly and will begin to engage it with greater rigor (see Zizek 1992). The student will see it wrapped in references to other symbols, other angles by which he or she can connect with it, dialogue with it, enlarge it, analyze it, revise it, and so on, just as he or she would when imaginitively engaged or suffused with what Dewey calls the "play attitude." Thus, a psychoanalytic pedagogy, like the ones Matthew Arnold and John Dewey derived from the Romantic model, would encourage students to engage language with increasing energy, to expand their sense of stylistic options and, in turn, their sense of options in their immediate social world. It would guard against a classroom situation in which words and texts are reduced to cold, opaque, alienating objects of egoistic fear and defeat, the sort of situation in which a writing assignment is perceived strictly as an opportunity for embarrassing, rock-chewing failure. Instead, it would seek to reawaken constantly the register in which words and texts are experienced as dynamic reservoirs of generative magic or desire.

For many teachers, however, the problem with any pleasure-based pedagogy, whether Romantic or psychoanalytic, is that it compromises the teacher's authority. There are perfectly good reasons why teachers today might be inclined to feel this way, for, as I noted, the most recent, widespread rendition of renegade rhetoric—the expressivism of the 1960s and '70s—was derived from the "self-actualization" psychologies of Jerome Bruner and Carl Rogers, and much of what Bruner and Rogers said about teaching inevitably proved quite troubling to those most ambitious in the field of rhetoric and composition, especially during the major phase of our professionalization in the 1980s.

"Self-Actualization," Solipsism, and Anarchy

In his 1969 collection of essays called *Freedom to Learn*, Carl Rogers recommends that a teacher should see him- or herself as a mere "facilitator," even as a "participant learner" whose first responsibility involves "setting the initial mood or climate" of the classroom through a form of "personal sharing" in which he or she "endeavors to recognize and accept his [or her] own limitations" (164–66). In *On Becoming a Person* (1961), he offers the following, quite shocking advice: because only learning is really important, not teaching, we should do away with grades, exams, degrees, perhaps even the whole institutional apparatus, for it can only interfere with the sort of learning that is most significant (277), the learning that renders people more flexible, more resilient, more joyful. Similarly, Jerome Bruner asserts that for students to learn they must only inhabit a certain kind of environment, that the formation of that environment marks the teacher's only responsibility, and, what's more, that this special environment resists technical understanding, for "people are not machines." Such remarks undoubtedly made possible a vulgar version of the Romantic-therapeutic classroom, one in which the best teachers were simply those most adept at "getting out of the way" of student self-discovery and self-expression, the ones most comfortable in an atmosphere in which "anything goes" and, most likely, nothing is learned.

However, Bruner nowhere describes the classroom environment he favors in terms of the emotionally effusive or the cozily permissive. Instead, he specifically describes it as an environment that makes available certain symbols by which the students can signal to themselves what they have achieved or what they intend to achieve (1966, 5, 28). More concretely, such a classroom might require students to compare their writings from earlier and later in the semester, track changes in the ways they perceive experiences or texts they've written about, or practice using stylistic devices until they become comfortable with them, for such requirements can help students undergo those sudden intellectual growth spurts in which they "know that they know," and which register as keen pleasure (27).

Bruner associates learning with a flash of inspiration in which the student forges from her surroundings a new means of addressing herself—a new depth, a new dignity. The student accesses a new identity in her community's "library of scripts." These moments of creative insight occur as rich surprise, as transgressions of the orderly categories by which the student formerly organized her sense of herself (18).[2] Bruner writes, "[The community contains] a corpus of images and identities and models that provides the pattern to which growth may aspire." More pointedly, he asserts, the "shape or style of a mind is, in some measure, the outcome of internalizing the functions inherent in the language we use" (107). Bruner insists not only that language plays an essential role in the development of selves, but also that it continues in this regard during moments of "inspiration" or pleasure: "When we are thinking at the far reach of our capacities, we are engaged with words, even led forward by them" (104).

Clearly, Bruner asks teachers to assume substantial responsibility. They must provide a model to which growth may aspire and make available to students powerful verbal techniques. He in no way favors the goals of solipsism and anarchy that many assume follow from "self-actualization" and that perhaps colored the classrooms of his less astute acolytes. His remarks about surprise, about personal transformation, and about the power of language would seem particularly well-suited to understanding Tharon's paper, and, for that matter, the ways we imagine our goals for all of our students and, most particularly, our own roles as teachers.

Similarly, while Carl Rogers (1961) affirms quite frequently the value of discovering what he calls one's "true self," he nowhere casts this entity, as so many have suggested, as anarchic or solipsistic. He insists not only that the "true self" is a fluid multiplicity, but also that, as such, it must constantly encounter and embrace that which is Other, and, in enjoying this very vital sort of self, one can't help but engage in creative activities like writing. For Rogers, the defining characteristic of all life is the "urge to expand, extend, develop, mature—the tendency to express and activate all the capacities of the organism"; and "as the organism forms new relationships to the environment in its endeavor most fully to be itself," it will engage in the work/play of the imagination (1961, 351). Again, the "true self" can only be realized in relationship with the Other. And Rogers thus implies that the teacher must do the difficult work of stimulating the imagination by playing the role of the Other for the student and fostering dialogue.[3]

Just as he celebrates a sense of self-as-process, a pluralistic "constellation of potentialities" (122) open to change and movement, Rogers also describes knowledge as dialogic and highly rhetorical: it must remain flexible, local, particular, pragmatic, and, above all, wholly experiential; it must remain rooted in the body's senses, desires, passions, exactly the ignoble domain, for Plato, to which rhetoric is restricted. Knowledge-as-rhetoric, for Rogers, is closer to lore and intuition than to the timeless truths discovered by philosophy, and thus teachers who adopt this perspective must remain very active and engaged, not withdrawn into the obscure heights of perfect mastery. Again, as with Bruner, I can't help but revisit these ideas as I wonder about Tharon's eroticized relation to knowledge about writing, his ongoing "courtship" with what he describes as a "necessary tool." I can't help but wonder how Rogers' and Bruner's ideas, and for that matter, Tharon's ideas, might shape my sense of the knowledge I want students to develop in my classroom and what all this means for my role as a teacher.

Unfortunately, many in composition assume that Bruner and Rogers and their expressivist descendants argue that teachers are largely irrelevant. And, as this vulgar version of "renegade rhetoric" has obscured subtler, more powerful versions, many have accused it, as we saw with Joseph Harris in Chapter 2, of an anti-intellectual, antiprofessional bias. By the late '80s and early '90s, in fact, part of what seemed to measure a rhetorician's degree of professionalism was his or her distance from the Romantic-therapeutic tradition, and, to the degree that writing teachers could scapegoat Romanticism and valorize its opposite (David Bartholomae's "academic discourse"), they could curry favor with—even win acceptance among—their literary colleagues. For they both, together, could thereby follow the noble lead of continental philosophy to make a heady sort of "social turn" away from the anecdotal lore about "inspiration" and the pleasures of personal voice that, they claimed, had characterized the work of the previous and not-yet-professionalized generation (see Gradin 1995, 11).

In order to rescue the renegade from the vulgar version and revive the possibility of a pleasure-based pedagogy, I'd like to conclude by detailing the rigors and responsibilities that I imagine for myself whenever I teach writing. In particular, I would like to explore how ideas about desire developed by psychoanalyst Jacques Lacan allow me to access and upgrade residual traces of the Romantic-therapeutic tradition among my students and initiate them into the joys of the sort so prized by Bruner, Rogers, and Tharon, joys that while neither solipsistic nor anarchic are nonetheless quintessentially renegade.

(Re)Inventing the Teacher

"The only genuine teaching," says Jacques Lacan, "is one which succeeds in awakening in those who are listening the desire to know." He adds, "This desire can only emerge when they themselves have taken the measure of ignorance as such" (1991b, 207). What Lacan means, I think, is quite similar to the advice of Bruner and Rogers: teachers must, paradoxically, commit themselves with utmost flexibility and sensitivity to the fine-grained, particular differences of each new classroom situation, that they must refuse any knowledge that would encumber their capacity to think on their feet, to improvise and engage students on the students' own, ever-evolving terms. Put simply, teachers need to know how to know—or, more pointedly, *how not to know*. This very tricky business of continuously cultivating a certain kind of ignorance in a way that will allow students to share in its generative power perhaps proceeds as the art of asking questions, questions that neither the students nor the teacher can readily answer; and, as soon as the teacher and student have worked together through their "ignorance" to a partial answer to the question, the teacher must undermine that answer with still more questions that are, again, more or less unanswerable. As a colleague of mine once put it, "I know I'm teaching at my best when I'm being too difficult *without* being too difficult." To borrow the terms of my second epigraph, this kind of teaching is corrosive, infernal, salutary, and medicinal. The teacher's insistent posing of problems and partial dismantling of his or her authority can trigger in students a keen desire to open themselves, in turn, to the work of generating and engaging new thoughts, of playing with these thoughts so happily that the ultimate goal of such play becomes only the endless continuation of the activity itself—an experience, no matter how fleeting, of eternity or the infinite.[4]

Consider, as well, that classroom activity I described in Chapter 1, in which students filled in words that conformed to the sequence of poetic devices that we had noted in some previous text; the way we produced a highly musical blob of nonsense that, in turn, became a powerful spur to interpretation and, yet more broadly, to the students' sensitivity to the ways sound or style undergirds "meaning." This sort of move, as I noted, counteracts the too-weighty vision of academic discourse as the voice of mastery, of the university as an alien monolith that can only humiliate student efforts at writing. It opens within the academy pathways for "ignorance," laughter, play, transgression, growth, and a very practical sort of critical savvy rooted in the sound of language, the cultivation of which has no endpoint.

Students generally find great pleasure in these sorts of classroom discussions and seem genuinely disappointed when the class period ends and we have to disband. They want the discussion to keep going. They seem to identify their pleasure not as a trivial sort of "feel-good" experience like eating a candy bar, but rather as the signal that something more serious is happening, something that, in its most extreme form, might have the power to heal, something that, as such, they can't help but love. In fact, I think that, as a teacher, I can succeed in this improvisational undermining of my authority, this performance of what Lacan describes as a certain kind of ignorance, to the degree that I can reflect upon, assume, speak through—and even manipulate—my own complicity in the currents of intersubjectivity, my own connection to that definitive spark of the renegade, the ever-evolving, endlessly decentering, and supremely social energy known as desire.

In other words, my job as a teacher is to foster an atmosphere that is not at all "free" or directionless, but rigorously engaged in the struggle to encounter, entertain, and work with ideas and perceptions that, at first, register as distinctly other, that, as such, can stimulate imagination and desire. Rather than simply try to "professionalize" myself by disavowing an allegedly naïve, pop-psychological enthusiasm for the domain of "feeling," I must always remind myself that "feeling"—or, more broadly, the felt, bodily experience of imagination and desire—forever spills into words and, from words, back into the imagining, desiring body. I must therefore model for students a certain kind of engagement with language, one keenly sensitive to the pleasures of stylistic play, the role of interpretation in the process of revision, and the power of interpretive, revisionary work to transform not simply the text but also the writer. To put it in simplest terms, I find that students have an uncanny knack for identifying where their teachers, as we say in New Orleans, *are at;* that is, they can see quickly how we feel about the experience of being in the classroom. And, all but instantaneously, they will begin to mimic us. To engage pedagogically this impulse to mimic is part of what it means to assume, take on, and analyze unconscious desire.

As Nicholas Delbanco (2002) argued in the pages of *Harper's*, mimicry is the oldest and most pervasive form of learning in the history of humankind, and so, whenever anyone must learn anything, their first move is to adopt models to imitate. And thus, in the writing classroom, students will unconsciously try to adopt, at least for a moment, their teacher's ways of looking at things, thinking about things, talking about things, and so on. If the teacher evinces little desire to communicate with students, the students will have considerable difficulty in summoning the desire to communicate with the teacher; the teacher's inaccessible authority, whether distanced from the students by hostility, laziness, or mere elitism, will become, when the students try to write, a rock to chew on, and those who succeed in the class will be those who manage to generate what, in all likelihood, they would secretly acknowledge as so much BS. Therefore, my ultimate responsibilities as a renegade teacher are continuous reflection that my students can imitate and a tireless dialogue with students that inquires into particular pieces of writing, how their particular rhetorical effects are achieved, whether and how such effects should be imitated.

Again, this sort of pedagogy deliberately engages unconscious desire. On one hand, this simply means that I must engage language with real energy. However, to do this well and to avoid burning out, to guide my reflections toward the goal of cultivating my desire and enabling it to spread contagiously among my students, I find that certain complex conceptual tools can prove invaluable as I reflect on my day-to-day interaction with students. To say it another way, I find that it helps in cultivating and renewing desire to know something of what desire is, and, in turn, how that web of identifications or imitations called the ego works to inhibit desire. With this sort of conceptual understanding, I think, all teachers can reflect on their classroom performances in ways that will energize them and, in turn, steer students away from the agonized, rock-chewing drudgery of coming up with meaningless drivel. Thus, while I offer in the appendix a handout on particular rhetorical strategies that I use with students, I will resist in this final section of the book any rigid prescriptions for classroom practice or curriculum design, for this is precisely the sort of dogma that the renegade must disavow, the sort of "knowledge" that, as we'll see, can ultimately lead students to so much miserable rock-chewing. Instead, I offer only some concepts that I keep in the back of my mind as I think on my feet in the classroom about how to help students enjoy writing.

With this understanding, teachers can reinvent themselves in the classroom, moment to moment, day by day, modeling for students the difficult work and highly pleasurable play of assuming and engaging unconscious desire. In so doing, teachers will create new experiential benchmarks of critical rigor and imaginative energy around which students' language can continue to orbit, quite joyfully, long after the class has ended.

The Teaching of Writing and the Psychoanalysis of Desire

Teaching, said Jacques Lacan, is a "function . . . to which I have truly devoted my entire life (quoted in Felman 1997, 21)," and he used the word *teaching*, according to Henry Sullivan (2002), in a very particular sense, for Lacan denied that he ever developed a theory *per se*, but rather only sought to accumulate, year by year, a protean body of teachings, and these teachings, this record of his performances, were very much about the art of teaching—what it is, how it works, how to do it, and so on. The connections, therefore, between teaching and pyschoanalysis are much simpler, argues Shoshana Felman, than they might first appear: we don't somehow "apply" or adapt or translate the concepts of the latter into those of the former; rather, we must come to understand how pedagogy, at its best, actually functions the way psychoanalysis does, how the methods and goals of each, ideally, overlap. This similarity between teaching and analysis has particular resonance for the teacher of writing, for when Lacan struggled toward the end of his career to identify what he had been doing for nearly forty years (is psychoanalysis a science? a philosophy? a religion?), he ultimately chose to consider his life's work a contribution to the tradition of rhetoric (Schneiderman 1983, 169). In other words, he saw himself as working against Plato's marginalization of rhetoric as the superficical stuff of mere desire and verbal manipulation by exploring the powerful dynamics between desire and style in the crucial human enterprises of healing and learning. As such, Lacan was deliberately returning to the Stoics and the sophists, pushing against Plato's division of body and soul just as Blake did. Moreover, this vision of teaching clearly echoes the ideas of Bruner and Rogers about eschewing finalized transcendent truths and about the value of offering students a certain kind of environment or set of models through which they can therapeutically self-actualize.[5]

Importantly, the psychoanalytically informed classroom does *not* require students to explore private memories of acute pain, for Lacan's interest, above all, is in strings of words. Thus, when writing teachers talk about style, they are also—implicitly, obliquely—addressing the depths of experience; and when students write about the depths of their experience, the teacher can continue to talk only about style. Even in those difficult instances when some students gravitate toward highly personal writing, the teacher need not become immersed in their private struggles the way many people assume that psychoanalysts do. For, as Mark Bracher argues (1999), even though such material likely impacts these students' relationship to language, and even though psychoanalytic concepts are the best tools we have for dealing with such material, Lacan asserted over and over that the principal object of inquiry for psychoanalysis (and thus for teachers who follow this model) is speech—that is, sequences of words, the more or less spontaneous, material action of human desire made manifest, moment to moment, within the abstract structures of language. Thus, the writing course informed by psychoanalysis continues to focus on texts, not necessarily the experience the text discusses.

The only experience that interests the teacher, in such a course, is the experience of writing and whether it becomes "inspired"—that is, whether it becomes infused with desire. Lacan's interest in speech can be translated into the contexts of the writing classroom, first, as an interest in the conversations that ensue between teachers and students, and also as an interest in style, for carefully crafted language, like speech, always wants to establish contact with an interlocutor, an audience. According to this view, both style and speech are dimensions of language that provide rich context for assuming and taking on—that is, tracing and analyzing—desire. As I noted in the second chapter, much this same interest has appeared in some of Peter Elbow's best work. Speech, says Elbow, is characterized by contextual immediacy, dialogic spontaneity, and rhythmic thrust, and so, too, is highly effective writing. If carefully stylized writing shares this same "energy" with speech, then the best teachers are the ones who can talk to their students in ways that will incite this energy within these conversations and, what's more, enable this energy to transpose itself into student writing. This, I think, is what Bruner and Rogers ask teachers to do, and I can't help but wonder if perhaps it explains some of what led Tharon to the sort the experience he describes.

This "energy," I must hasten to add, is not easy to define: as Jean Laplanche and Jean-Bertrand Pontalis (1973) put it, the concept of desire is simply so fundamental to the discourse of psychoanalysis that it cannot be defined in full. Nonetheless, a working definition: if all creatures that are conscious are, at some level or another, conscious of the possibility of not being conscious (that is, of dying), then they must repress this awareness of their mortality in order to get on with the business of surviving as long as possible. This repression takes the form of an insatiable hunger for physical presence, for Being, and this hunger Lacan calls desire. Take, for example, those awful moments when class discussion seems lifeless, even punctuated by long, dreadful silences: what makes these moments so distasteful is that this silence is roughly analogous to that void that desire forever seeks to fill, and, insofar as this void is not filled, desire is thwarted, and discomfort burgeons.

In order to fill this primordial void, desire posits an endless array of objects, but its ultimate object must remain something that it can never actually attain, for the objects it posits mostly serve as dangling carrots, as stimuli that can never fall within desire's grasp. Desire, then, is a process, and the elusive, illusory objects it casts in its path (and through which it constitutes its path and, in turn, itself) are symbols, and, most often, words. This way of thinking about desire explains why, as I noted in Chapter 1, the renegade tradition has chosen to cast the pleasures of writing always in terms of the *process* of writing: when writing is viewed as a process it can become suffused with that more primary and all-powerful process, desire, and lead to moments, however fleeting, of pleasure.

To say it another way, desire is to symbols as a spider is to the silk it spins. And we might suppose that the formal symmetry of the spider's web, the balanced, repetitive architecture the spider creates, the structure through which the spider captures food and creates a general, self-aware sense of "home," is called the ego. This laboriously constructed signature, this keystone or linchpin to one's self-image radiates outward like spokes from a wheel and generates one's entire fantasy of symmetry, balance, and cohesion, which, in turn, allows one to negotiate one's experience of space and cultivate a certain sense of one's own consistency over time. This concept of the ego explains why students sometimes "resist" our pedagogies or grumble about having to revise their essays: the work we ask them to do pushes them to see key aspects of that web of identifications called the ego in ways that threaten it.

When the ego is challenged, it responds with an obstinacy that repeats, usually in miniature, a version of the rage and terror that colored its initial formation. More specifically, the ego emerges in infancy as a moment of primal trauma or symbolic "castration" and sparks the acquisition of language, for while infants (from the Latin, meaning "without speech") initially draw no distinction between their own body and that of their mother, there eventually comes a moment when the infant witnesses this other body as having coherence, integrity, coordination, and distinction; and this moment—a chaotic jumble of fear, envy, betrayal, and a desperate impulse to mimic—initiates the child into the Imaginary or Mirror stage; this stage (pun intended) persists as a mode of mental activity throughout life, as Mark Bracher puts it, as a fund of "imagistic memory and codes, a sense of visual-spatial orientation and a sense of bodily coherence and integration" that is forever beseiged by the nostalgic desire to return to the oceanic joys of the earlier dimension (1999, 25), to reverse this primal trauma, in an apotheosis of eternity or the infinite.

Indeed, when our writing is relatively filled with pleasure, we have somehow managed to loosen the structures of the ego, to suspend the ego, even dissolve it in a quasi-erotic contact with the Other, a contact we experience as especially "clear" communication. Conversely, when the ego feels threatened, it reasserts itself in ways that block this possibility. This is perhaps the primary insight around which the renegade classroom is organized, and of course, the essential trick of such a classroom is to disarm the ego without letting it feel threatened, without triggering an explosion.[6]

To deconstruct the ego, it helps to know a little more about how it develops. Despite the antagonism of desire, the ego increasingly emerges, within the Imaginary phase, as a vision of the solid, formal architecture or symmetry of one's body, in which it sees itself as a kind of defining, microcosmic, quintessential core that distills all fear, envy, betrayal, and idealizing mimicry into a perfect gem of misery. As the Imaginary persists as a particular dimension throughout our lives, the ego, as the central fantasy or, more precisely, the fantasy of a center, continues to collect innumerable, onion-like layers of identifications with idealized authorities—teachers, parents, older siblings, celebrities—whose place the ego wishes to usurp, but cannot. In this sense, the ego is a crown that never quite fits, because it has always been borrowed from someone else. If the ego were to vanquish and supplant its models, as it wishes, it would no longer have these models upon which to rely and through which to focus itself. In this sense, the ego is intrinsically self-defeating, self-punishing, for it forever seeks to devour and supplant that which is the very basis of its existence. As Lacan puts it in *Seminar I*, the ego is "structured like a symptom, the human symptom par excellence, the mental illness of man" (1991, 16). To revert to the terms I used in Chapter 1, the ego is the substance of masochism. And therefore it is the secret target of "corrosive, medicinal" teaching, for as we loosen the boundaries of the ego and open the student to an experience of selves, texts, and worlds as dynamic, interanimating processes, we heighten the student's capacity for critical reflection, we stir desire and prepare the way for pleasure.

Conversely, the maintenance of the ego is difficult, distasteful work, an always masochistic undertaking, what my students would call BS and what Lacan would call "empty speech": an awkward, parroted patchwork of cliché, tortured syntax, and high-sounding, mishandled diction, an unintentional parody of the voice of authority.

Consider, for example, the student who has begun to construct teachers as an overly lofty ego-ideal and who therefore strives to imitate the kind of discourse that he or she thinks the teacher, as an academic, will favor. This student will often produce the written equivalent of empty speech and will likely feel deeply embarrassed, even angry and defiant, when shortcomings in his or her essay are pointed out. Or consider those students who are so intimidated by the prospect of communicating with the teacher that, in their writing, they retreat into vague clichés and simplistic structures like the five-paragraph theme: this is another brand of empty speech, one that seeks only to assert that which is too vague and too general to be contested, too simple to solicit active engagement.

As I noted in Chapter 3, my students do *not* feel that producing the written equivalent of empty speech offers any pleasure. On the contrary, they expressed a keen dislike for generating such BS, for this is the work of repression, the disavowal of desire, the ultimately futile and masochistic struggle to bolster or protect the ego. Consider in these terms that student who said that writing an essay for school was like chewing on a rock: so awestruck is this student by the power and remoteness of the world of school that his attempts to communicate within it are arid and useless, almost a form of choking. In fact, this rock is the perfect metaphor for the ego, which, in feeling supremely threatened, reasserts its presence with extraordinary solidity and weight; it is imitating the principal object upon which it is transfixed, the alien monolith, the black hole, the kernel of terror, that, for this student, is school.

When I emphasize matters of prose style in my writing pedagogy, I implicitly try to lead students in the opposite direction—toward writing that is analogous to what Lacan calls "full speech." This sort of language doesn't disavow desire to bolster the ego; on the contrary, this language constantly reinterprets itself, and, in so doing, it assumes, takes on, analyzes, and cultivates unconscious desire. More concretely, my pedagogy insistently directs students to consider alternate phrasings and to wonder about which one feels best. In so doing, it allows desire to keep producing and playing with new symbolic configurations. I described much this same practice at the end of Chapter 2 in the context of the primitive and the doubles, an approach to writing that privileges questions of style and the felt sense.

By asking teachers to promote this sort of inward dialogue in students, I'm not simply privileging self-indulgence. On the contrary, at least since Kenneth Bruffee's work in the mid-'80s on collaborative learning, if not Paulo Freire's *Pedagogy of the Oppressed* in 1970, many composition teachers have likely surmised that when they talk with students about individual sentences and paragraphs, the students can gradually internalize this back-and-forth dynamic. And, as the students' capacity for inward dialogue grows, they come to feel increasingly comfortable with the act of critical reflection. For example, when I discuss, say, grammatical error, as a rhetorical problem that spoils the space of intersubjective connection between reader and writer, I hope to teach much more successfully than when I simply mark it with a red pen and tell the student to "fix" it. In other words, I never seek to cultivate student pleasure with liberationist slogans like "Don't worry about the rules! Just relax and be yourself!" On the contrary, I try to cast errors as carrying a certain generative force, as an opportunity for inward reflection about what might sound or feel better. For these reasons, I never require a student who is having trouble, say, with run-on sentences, to memorize the definitions of independent and dependent clauses and what the rules are for joining and punctuating them. On the contrary, I ask them how it feels to read a particular stretch of words in one part of the draft as compared to another stretch elsewhere, how the two strings of words differ, how one might sound or feel better than the other. This view of error, I think, is commensurate with what Lacan describes as the generative power of ignorance.

I want my students to learn that whenever they feel a twinge of discomfort or anxiety about a moment in their prose, a break or rupture in the language, they should engage those moments productively and treat them as places where something new or heretofore undisclosed is on the verge of breaking into view. As Nancy Welch puts it in *Getting Restless: Rethinking Revision and Writing Instruction* (1997), an *ethical* practice of revision, an honest and generous practice of revision, is one in which the dissonant aspects of a text are not simply dropped out but opened up and explored for the rich possibilities they may be engendering (2). When I emphasize with students the power of dialogue this way, I not only promote the habit of critical reflection and interpretation—I also lead students beyond the misery and alienation of the ego to the realm of unconscious desire, and, by creating this sort of pathway, I allow them to assume or "take on" desire, to analyze it, and, in turn, to move toward the experience of pleasure.

In order to foster this experience in the classroom, I try to model for my students an awareness of the general structure of dialogue. This structure, which we all intuitively grasp well before we reach adulthood, is such that, at the end of the subject's statement, the Other's after-the-fact determination of what the speaker said actually dictates, in a sense, the meaning of the statement. The subject makes the statement, but the message is chosen and constructed by the Other. To say this another way, the meaning of any string of words is always up for grabs until the final word has been spoken and then heard and determined by the listener, at which point the whole meaning of the string becomes complete, whereupon its significance suddenly looms much larger. This is why, in any debate, each participant wants to have the last word. More abstractly, the question always floating underneath any chain of utterances is "what will this have meant?" And the ongoing chain of utterances that shapes one's day-to-day life constantly poses the same question, a kind of unconscious, insistent desire for interpretation or analysis: "what will this have meant?" At its most pressing, this question can prompt people to undertake professional psychoanalysis, but, of course, it can only be answered in full upon that person's death and only by someone else.

In the writing classroom, however, something like a miniature death intervenes upon one's stream of utterances whenever one hazards a partial answer to the perennial question of "what will this have meant?" Whenever one engages in interpretation or analysis, one doesn't simply look into an earlier stretch of symbols and alter them to rewrite history, but, in so doing, one also shapes the future direction of the signifying chain, thereby performing a prophetic or magical act. What's more, this act carries a certain physical sense of release, a twinge of pleasure or *jouissance*, an experience in which the ego as imagistic memory and codified precedent is washed away and we feel as though we're making genuine contact with the realm of sheer Being/Becoming: we call this quasi-erotic, "eureka" moment simply "insight." An insight is a "moment of truth" or a "moment of clarity," and it can occur as a minor observation or a cathartic, transfiguring revelation, depending on the context and the sort of dialogue, the particular habits of interpretation that the teacher has modeled for the student. Again, miniature versions of this pleasure occur when writers tinker with sentences and ask questions about how a particular configuration feels to them, how it might be made to feel better.

I want to sensitize my students to the fact that their pleasure and mine, as well as our knowledge and authority, are a function of dialogue, a function of this "excess" of signifiers. More specically, I want them to realize that we are always mobilizing many more signifiers than we can know, emitting signs that invite interpretations that far exceed our particular intentions. In this sense, our "knowledge" always carries with it a certain excess about which we are mostly ignorant—or, to use the precise psychoanalytic term, "unconscious." This ignorance, says Felman, is not simply "opposed to knowledge: it is itself a radical condition, an integral part of the very structure of knowledge" (1997, 25). This ignorance is best understood as a passion to ignore, to repress, and resist; and the purpose of knowing, in this light, becomes seeking out these patterns of resistance, interpreting them, to see what this "ignorance" can reveal and teach.

This particular purpose can guide the composing process quite successfully, especially in the writer's imagining of his or her audience, about whom the writer is always largely "ignorant." Even though this ignorance—the ego's resistance to unconscious desire—is powerful, it is not quite as powerful as desire itself. No one can keep the unconscious locked away in a vault. Instead, we "transfer" or project it onto certain deeply authoritative, even emblematic figures whom we encounter in the social world, figures who come to serve among our ego identifications and thereby contain unconscious desire and secretly shape, in turn, our sense of audience when we write. We seek to control our interaction with these figures as fully as possible, but, of course in so doing, we enter into a dialogue with them, and, through these emblems of the unconscious, we enter into dialogue with the voice of unconscious desire itself—with that which forever slides beyond the defenses of the ego to become the discourse of the Other. Of course, in general terms, how the person upon whom the transference is directed chooses to act will have enormous bearing on how the person doing the transferring will experience the unconscious. In the context of the writing classroom, therefore, enormous responsibility falls on the shoulders of the teacher.

As a teacher, I cannot simply transmit the substance of knowledge to the students in the hopes that they will contain it. On the contrary, my knowledge "is not a substance but a structural dynamic" and therefore "Dialogue is thus the radical condition of learning and knowledge, the analytically constitutive condition through which ignorance becomes structurally informative" (Felman 1997, 29). For my pedagogy to work, I must relinquish the role of the authoritative master of all there is to know about writing. Instead, for me, the art of teaching becomes the art of asking questions that are not readily answerable, the art by which the student and I work together through the ignorance, the unconscious desire that we share, assuming it and analyzing it as it manifests itself in how we feel about particular verbal configurations. This is the "corrosive, medicinal" work of assuming and analyzing desire. It dismantles the ego's authority, disassembles its layers of idealized images, and plays with and against the eternally springing mechanism of transference/repression.

When I feel threatened as a teacher by these processes, my ego authoritatively reasserts itself, inducing in students a corresponding, egoistic fear and alienation in which the intersubjective space of desire or transference becomes a no-man's-land, a desolate, even dangerous dimension to close down as quickly as possible. If this becomes the dominant mood of the class, my students will write poorly. The opposite mode is the ongoing celebration of the unconsious, the intersubjective space that is constituted in the excess of signifiers. This is exactly the way of framing pedagogy that I described in the first chapter in conjunction with those revolutionaries who cut a hole in their flag, for it associates academic discourse, for example, not with a position of absolute mastery but rather with something like a subculture, a position in steady critical dialogue with dominant mechanisms of repression. Shoshana Felman calls this knowledge and teaching "literary" for it recalls the point Socrates made about poets: they do not write their poetry from any sort of wisdom, says Socrates, but rather by genius or inspiration; not from philosophic or intellectual mastery, but from the knowledge that they cannot know completely all of what they are writing. In short, poets *know*, but they never quite know the full meaning of what they know. They remain in dialogue with open-ended possibility, and, as such, they are the greatest teachers and precisely the sort of model that teachers should strive to become for their students of writing.

This philosophy helps me teach students how to write, train other people to become writing teachers, and develop a body of scholarly work within the discipline of rhetoric and composition. However, it resists any sort of lockstep recipe. For, alas, what I advocate is only a certain position in regard to style and desire in the classroom, and whether we call this position "renegade" or "inspired" or "literary" or "rhapsodic" or "sublime" or "corrosive" or "therapeutic," this position does not simply emphasize questions of prose style but, again, models a radicalized relation to the whole domain of style: style as the milieu through which one forever reinterprets words in search of words that feel more felicitous; style as that which resists finalized descriptions and prescriptions that would dominate and totalize in the name of absolute mastery; style as a dimension of the composing process in which one proceeds with the knowledge that one's meaning can never be determined but by some other; style, then, as a way of welcoming opposition, alterity, Otherness, and thereby conjuring the very embodiment of unconscious desire as that which has no limits, as that which is infinite. To adopt this position is to embrace magic and to experience, finally, what my student, Tharon McDowell, identified as the "creator": writing.

Though this experience might seem impossibly remote from the group of students one may face on Monday morning, I hope that the concrete strategies, intellectual traditions, and conceptual tools I've sketched here will provide teachers with the resources they need to engage and cultivate the student's capacity for composing pleasure. I hope too that what I offer here will help resolve our field's recent, bitter disputes between those who advocate academic discourse and those more interested in personal voice. Finally, I hope that it will help us honor the age-old, "conservative" mission to get students to write more clearly by keeping in play the most contrary, subversive, and complex insights our inquiry into language has ever produced. In sum, I think our profession can find in this renegade tradition its future: style as the ongoing renewal of desire, writing as the practice of the pleasure. I think a good number of my students have come to a similar sort of understanding, and I plan to expand the stylistic components of my pedagogy considerably in the future, for it seems to have solved key problems and provided keen pleasures.

Notes

1. See Gradin 23–28, as well as Roskelly and Ronald (1998)and my own essay in the Fall 1998 issue of *Composition Studies* (26.2). My own immersion as an undergraduate and an MA student in the most radical stands of English Romanticism—specifically, the major prophecies of William Blake—first generated the preoccupations that ultimately positioned me to write this book. In fact, in earlier drafts of it, I went to great lengths to argue for the centrality of Blake to the renegade tradition and to delineate uncanny correspondences between some of Blake's ideas and those in Tharon's paper. This work increasingly seemed to digress into hermeneutics and theology, however, and to disrupt my primary mission of reflecting on how I teach writing. Nonetheless, I would urge anyone interested in themes of the infinite, the imagination, the body, and writing to visit Blake's universe.

2. As such, Bruner was a key source in the early 1960s for composition's discussion of writing as a process, its revolt against literary models and overmuch concern about final textual products. Moreover, he also echoes Blake's remarks about writing with corrosive acids.

3. As William Blake put it in *The Marriage of Heaven and Hell*, "Opposition is true friendship."

4. This is essentially what Paulo Freire prized as education for critical consciousness. What's more, as Jerome McGann (1973) suggests, this is the primary purpose of William Blake's major prophecies.

5. Lacan was famously opposed to, even bitterly critical of American ego-psychology and defined his life's work, in large measure, in terms of rescuing the Freudian legacy from the American concept of self and returning the work of psychoanalysis to its proper interest, the symbolic mechanisms of the unconscious. Despite this conflict, I'm inclined to see Bruner and Rogers' ideas of self-actualization as thoroughly analogous to the Lacanian project of assuming unconscious desire, for they are both projects that seek to avail the human subject of the pleasures that derive from an experiences of the self and of language as dynamically intertwined processes. In other words, their conflict, despite the way disciples of Bruner and Rogers might have conceived of the self, is a surface matter of intellectual politics and, in fact, their ideas are not ultimately opposed.

6. For a beautiful description of how this sort of experience can unfold within writers, see Barrett Mandel's 1980 essay, "The Writer Writing Is Not at Home."

Appendix

Stylistic Principles
and Devices

When you revise your papers, I want you to think very deliberately about eight different stylistic principles: transition, clarity, emphasis, balance, figurative language, syntax, restatement, and sound. These principles have been identified by Robert Harris as essential elements of style. When you look closely at your sentences and paragraphs with these principles in mind, you'll find that they allow you to see, quite objectively, where your prose is strongest and where it is weakest. Try to develop the habit of using these principles to revise your prose.

With each of the broad principles that I describe, you'll find several devices that can help you fulfill the particular principle. Think of these devices as verbal patterns or forms or "tricks" that can make your prose more graceful, more powerful, and more memorable. Think of some of them, on one hand, as ornaments, as a means to take what you've said and recast it in ways that your readers will enjoy. On the other hand, working with these ornaments can also stimulate your imagination— that is, as you work to reshape certain moments in your paper to fit these formulae, you may find all sorts of new ideas popping up. So, as you revise your papers with these devices (and, too, with an awareness of the broad principles that these devices help you fulfill), be open to the possible emergence of wholly new material.

These devices are quite powerful. Many of them were first organized more than two thousand years ago in ancient Greece, and they have had an extraordinary influence on the ways we've used language ever since. Most of the information that follows I've taken from three books—*A Handlist of Rhetorical Terms* by Richard Lanham, *Writing with Clarity and Style* by Robert Harris, and *Style* by Joseph Williams—all of which I heartily recommend, for they've helped my own writing enormously. Some of these devices have fairly exotic names, but don't be intimidated or put off by them: I'm not especially concerned about whether you learn to pronounce or spell these names correctly. Also, don't feel as though you have to memorize them; instead, I want you to become familiar with these devices as tools that can give you more and more control over your prose, and, in turn, more and more success communicating with your readers.

One last point by way of introduction, one that's *very, very important:* don't get hung up trying to fulfill these formulae before you know what you want to say! Rather, after you've done some brainstorming and have a general sense of the ideas and details you want to engage in your paper, then—and only then—should you start trying to make certain moments in your paper fulfill some of these formulae. By the same token, you might find that if you can't come up with ideas that you need for your paper, playing around with some of these devices can help generate ideas for writing.

Transitions

We will nearly always make our readers happiest when we give them writing that "flows." But how do you make a piece of writing "flow"? Here is a paragraph that, as Joseph Williams notes, doesn't flow particularly well.

> Some astonishing questions about the nature of the universe have been raised by scientists exploring black holes in space. The collapse of a dead star into a point perhaps no larger than a marble creates a black hole. So much matter pressed into so little volume changes the fabric of space around it in puzzling ways. My favorite movie of all time actually deals with the issues surrounding black holes. (99)

Here is how Williams revised the paragraph to make it flow a little better:

> Some astonishing questions about the nature of the universe have been raised by scientists exploring black holes in space. A black hole is created when a dead star collapses into a point perhaps no larger than a marble. Because black holes compress so much matter into such small volume, the fabric of space around them changes in puzzling ways. The issues surrounding black holes are actually dealt with in one of my all-time favorite movies.

What changed? Why does the second version seem better? The words are virtually the exact same in both versions, but the words in the second version are presented in a slightly different order. Each sentence begins with references to black holes, and this concept was introduced in the very first sentence. Therefore, each sentence begins by grounding itself in something that the reader will feel is familiar. Also, each sentence ends by introducing the reader to something new ("a point perhaps no larger than a marble;" "puzzling ways;" "all-time favorite movies"). This steady movement within each sentence from the old to the new, from the familiar to the unfamiliar is the essence of "flow." In the first version, the opposite is true: that paragraph doesn't flow very well because every time the readers start a new sentence, they find themselves on unfamiliar territory and without any immediate sense of continuity. After you've drafted a paper, get in the habit of checking it for flow. Just look at the beginning and the ending of each sentence, and make sure that each one begins on a familiar note and ends on an unfamiliar note.

A concept closely related to flow is called *focus*. When writing is incoherent or unfocused, the reader will often simply quit reading. In order to prevent such breakdowns between reader and writer, the writer must make certain to sustain a focus. A paragraph will be well focused if each sentence begins with a topic that fits with the other topics announced in other sentences in that paragraph. In short, a paragraph is focused if it has a consistent string of topics. Here is an example, adapted from Williams, of a paragraph that flows smoothly but has no focus:

> Saner, Wisconsin is the snowmobile capital of the world. The buzzing of snowmobile engines fills the air, and their tanklike tracks crisscross the snow. The snow reminds me of Mom's mashed potatoes, covered with furrows I would draw with my fork. Mom's mashed potatoes usually made me sick, that's why I was playing with them. I like to make a hole in the middle of the potatoes and fill it with gravy. This behavior often made my little brother laugh. But, really, making my little brother laugh isn't very hard. He laughs at everything, because he's crazy. (103)

Notice the problem here: the paragraph is not focused on a single topic, but rather jumps from Wisconsin to snowmobile engines to snow to mashed potatoes to a certain kind of behavior to a little brother. In other words, each sentence sets forth a different topic. In order to revise that passage, the writer needs to isolate a central theme and make sure that each sentence begins with a topic that directly echoes that central theme, like this:

> Saner, Wisconsin, is the snowmobile capital of the world. All winter, the woods around Saner buzz with the sound of snowmobile engines, and the Saner snow is always criss-crossed with their tanklike tracks. Saner snowmobilers love to go home to a big meal after a day in the woods, and a great many of them have fallen in love with my mom's mashed potatoes and gravy. We would stuff ourselves with those potatoes, then plan an evening of night races in the woods, much to the delight of my easily amused—indeed, crazy—younger brother.

Notice the consistency in the string of topics: "Saner" and then "woods around Saner" and then "Saner snow" and then "Saner snowmobilers" and finally "we." Near the beginning of each sentence, a topic is set forth that relates quite closely to the other topics in the other sentences. One more example: if you were reading a paragraph in which the first sentence presents, near its very beginning, the topic of airplanes, and then the next sentence offers the topic of trains, and the third one cars, you know you're in a paragraph that is focused on transportation. But if, in the fourth sentence, the topic that emerges at the opening of the sentence is waterbugs, we know the paragraph is suddenly losing focus.

> Airplanes make an extraordinary amount of noise. Trains, on the other hand, aren't so bad. Some cars are quite noisy, too, but happily they are required by law to have a muffler. Waterbugs may or may not make a noise, but since I don't live near water, I cannot say for sure.

When the reader gets to that last sentence, the focus collapses and the reader suddenly begins to feel significantly confused. If that last sentence began by mentioning "the noise pollution caused by modern transportation" or if it began by mentioning something closely related to that theme, the sentence would be fine—even if it ultimately took up issues relating to waterbugs.

Here's the point: If a paragraph offers, from one sentence to the next, a string of closely related topics, the paragraph will be well focused. If one or more of the topics seems not to fit, then, at exactly that point, the focus will seem to wobble or blur or even disappear altogether. To check your work for focus, simply look at the topics of sentences and ask yourself if they constitute a consistent set. If not, revise the paragraph until the topics are consistent. Although this method works well for testing the focus of a particular paragraph, it can also be used to test the overall focus of an entire essay. Simply look at the topic that is announced at the beginning of each paragraph, and then decide if any of the topics are too far away from the main topic. If one is "off," fix it so that it fits with the others.

In addition to these broad principles of flow and focus, you can make strong transitions in your writing by using what Robert Harris calls logical connectors: these are words or phrases that connect one stretch of material (a sentence or paragraph) to another by relying on particular forms of logic. These forms of logic, says Harris, are Addition, Comparison, Contrast, Time, Purpose, Place, and Result (36). For example, one stretch of material might essentially function as an addition to an earlier stretch, and so you can introduce this paragraph, let's say, with phases like, "A further X . . ." or "Another X . . ." or "Too . . ." or "Also . . ." or "In addition to. . . ." If you'll notice, the paragraph you're reading right now used exactly this latter sort of logical connector in order to begin smoothly and with a strong transition out of the preceding paragraph.

Just as the logic of addition can tighten your transitions, so too can the logic of comparison. If a new paragraph serves as a comparison to the stuff you wrote about in the preceding paragraph, you might begin this new paragraph with phrases like, "A similar X . . ." or "Just as X, so too X . . ." or "Another version of X . . . ." This paragraph you are reading right now, by the way, began with a transition that relied on precisely this logic of comparison.

The opposite sort of logic can help with transitions—that of contrast. If the new material is meant to function in contrast to the material that just preceded it, you might begin that new paragraph with transitional phrases like "And yet . . ." or "But another . . ." or "Otherwise . . ." or "On the other hand . . ." or "The opposite. . . ." Again, this very paragraph you're reading right now used this latter sort of logical connector to smooth the transition from the preceding paragraph.

There are many other logical connectors. Some rely on the logic of time: if the material in a new paragraph involves events that have occurred after the events in a previous paragraph, you might begin that new paragraph with words like "After . . ." or "Later. . . ." If the temporal sequence is different, obviously you'll want to use different words like "Before" or "Earlier" or "Now" or "Soon" or "Meanwhile" or some other word or phrase. These words all use the logic of time to connect sentences and paragraphs. Other logical connectors might use purpose, such as "Because of this, President Bush chose . . ." Or "For these reasons, we must agree that. . . ." Others might use the logic of place ("Beyond" or "Nearby" or "In front of") and, finally, others might use the logic of result ("And so" or "Then" or "In consequence . . ."). By the way, can you tell which sort of logical connector I used to make a smooth transition into this paragraph?

There are also five powerful **verbal devices** you can use to help with the transitions in your paper:

Procatelpsis—This device for making transitions anticipates an objection or counterargument that some readers might raise and responds to it. For example, "While some may insist that my interpretation of *Hamlet* ignores important features of the play, those features of the play only become important if one is committed to an interpretation that distorts Shakespeare's ultimate message." This sort of device is virtually essential to a successful argumentative paper, and, when used well, it can help create an almost conversational tone, as if the writer were creating a lively, spontaneous dialogue with those who might disagree with his or her point. I strongly recommend that you grow comfortable using this device to make transitions in your argumentative writing.

Hypophora—This device for making transitions, as Harris says, involves asking one or more questions and then proceeding to answer them, usually at some length. The most common usage is to ask a question at the beginning of a paragraph, and then devote the remainder of the paragraph to answering the question. This device can work especially well in the latter stages of your paper, when you've already said enough that your position naturally raises certain questions that you can then identify and answer. Like procatelpsis, this is a great way to create a conversational tone in your essay (33).

Metabasis—This is a brief statement that sums up what has already been said and what will follow. For example, "Thus, I've proven that *Hamlet* is not necessarily the most perfect of Shakespeare's tragedies, and now I need to prove why *Macbeth* is." Obviously, in a short paper, this device will rarely be useful. This device is primarily useful toward the middle of longer essays.

Anadiplosis—This device repeats the last word of one clause to begin the next one. Here is one of Harris' examples: "Students need to respect the rules, rules that were invented for the students' own good." Or, "This treatment plant has a record of reliability, a reliability envied by all other treatment plants of its kind in the nation." This device is especially useful for helping your prose to flow smoothly (111).

Conduplicatio—This device is very similar to anadiplosis, but, instead of repeating the last word to begin a new clause or sentence, this device just repeats a *key* word from the preceding clause or sentence, as in "Some people love taking online courses through the University New Orleans, and, indeed, online courses are gaining in popularity throughout the United States." Again, this device is useful in making your prose flow smoothly.

Clarity

The human mind loves to process information in the form of a story. Indeed, whenever it is presented with particularly complex material, one of its first steps is to turn the material into a dynamic event that stars a character and an action. For these reasons, readers prefer sentences to foreground a character and an action, and the sooner in a sentence the reader finds a character followed by an action, the happier the reader will be (see Williams 1999, 42–44). Consider, for example, how horrible this sentence is: "Once upon a time, a walk through the woods by Little Red Riding Hood was occurring, when a jump-out from behind a tree by The Big Bad Wolf caused fright in her." What makes that sentence so awful is that the main characters are not up front in the subject-position where they belong and their main actions are obscured by the fact that they are not expressed in the verb position. Consider how much better this version is: "Once upon a time, Little Red Riding Hood was walking through the woods, when the The Big Bad Wolf jumped out from behind a tree and frightened her." This sentence is better because it foregrounds character and action, and, more specifically, because it puts the character in the subject-position and the action in the verb-position. Here's another example from Joseph Williams: "The loss of market share to Japan by American auto-manufacturers resulted in the loss of employment by hundreds of thousands of factory workers in Detroit and a decline in the general economy of the upper midwest" (56). To improve this sentence, we first need to identify the main characters (American auto-manufacturers, Detroit factory workers, the upper midwest's economy) and then identify their main actions (lost market shares to Japan, lost their jobs, declined). And then we can rewrite the sentence to put these characters and their actions in the prominent positions where readers want them, like this: "When American auto-manufacturers lost a share of the market to Japan, hundreds of thousand of Detroit factory workers lost their jobs and the upper midwest's economy declined."

In addition to this principle of character-and-action, **here are a number of powerful devices** you can use to make your message clearer:

Distinctio—This device might also be called simply "definition." You can make your prose clearer by defining important words that might otherwise remain ambiguous. Here is how Harris illustrates this device: "It is impossible to make gasoline that costs twenty-five cents a gallon—by *impossible* I mean currently beyond our present technological abilities" (39). This device is invaluable when you're arguing about ideas that are relatively abstract, for it allows you to pause and make these abstractions more concrete and less ambiguous. Remember, however, that you should only use this device when a particular word is both important and potentially ambiguous. Again, it is extremely useful when constructing an argument.

Exemplum—This device for clarifying what you mean might also be called simply "example." As Harris notes, examples often include *visual* details, for readers love to process information not only in stories, as I noted above, but as *pictures* (41). Whenever your material is relatively abstract, try to use an exemplum—that is, offer a quick picture, a visual version of what you mean, to help your reader grasp what you're saying. You might also use the exemplum to provide specifics that will concretize your more general idea; here is an example from Harris, "The conifers (evergreens like pine and cypress trees) produce seeds in hard, cone-shaped structures" (41). Notice how "evergreen" offers something like a picture, and "pine and cypress" offer particular details to concretize what you're talking about.

Amplification—This device, says Harris, consists of restating a word and adding a little more detail (42). This sort of repetition not only clarifies but draws attention and emphasis to something that might otherwise be passed over too casually by the reader. Here is Harris' example: "In my hunger after ten days of overly rigorous dieting, I saw visions of ice cream—mountains of creamy, luscious ice cream, chocolate and vanilla, dripping with gooey hot fudge syrup and many millions of calories." Notice how this second half of the sentence simply repeats "ice cream" and adds lots of visual detail and particular meaning. The reader no longer passes casually over the point that the dieter was having visions of ice cream; rather the reader almost shares those visions and therefore appreciates how much they mean to the writer.

Metanoia—This device, says Harris, qualifies a statement or a part of statement by rejecting it or calling it back and expressing it in a better way, either more strongly or more mildly or just differently (43). For example, "The most important aspect of a reed for a tenor saxophone is its hardness; no, not its hardness so much as its inner strength. You certainly don't want one that's brittle." This device clarifies, of course, but it also gives emphasis and a tone of spontaneity and conversational directness. Here is another example: "The new gym on campus will improve the fitness level of our faculty and students, or rather the whole well-being, physical *and mental*, of everyone who uses it." Certain sorts of phrases are useful in building a metanoia: "I mean. . ." or "More precisely. . ." or "Or maybe. . . ."

Emphasis

Not every word in a given piece of writing is as important as every other word, and therefore successful writers make certain to place their most important words where these words will get the sort of rhythmic thrust that they deserve. A successful writer knows that even when readers are silently reading they still "feel" a certain rhythmic emphasis at the very beginning of each sentence and an even stronger one at the very end of every sentence. Notice how, as Joseph Williams explains, when you read this sentence out loud, your voice drops a little after the first word ("notice") and then rises again rather dramatically at the end, like this (122):

> NOTICE how
> As you as you read this sentence out loud, your voice . . . and then
> RISES AGAIN
> rather DRAMATICALLY at **THE END**

Did you catch that extra emphasis falling on the word "end"? Again, these rhythms influence our sense of what's most important in a sentence even when we're reading in silence. Therefore, the successful writer knows that she must put only the most important words at the ends of her sentences, and, at the beginnings of sentences, she should use words that are also worthy of the special rhythmic thrust.

Consider, for example, these pairs of sentences that I adapted from Joseph Williams (124):

> I suppose that the evidence that UFOs have actually visited our planet is not very convincing to me for the most part.

> I'm not much convinced by the evidence that our planet has been visited by UFOs.

Most readers will find the second one of the pair much more effective, for the first one has a lot of words that are not relatively important in positions of emphasis. The second one, however, puts only the most important words in those emphatic positions. See if you can tell the difference in the following pair:

> Sociobiologists suggest that our genes control our social behavior in the ways we behave around other people every day of our lives.

> Sociobiogists suggest that our genes control our social behavior.

As Harris notes, some go so far as to say that writers should make sure that the first syllable of every sentence should have a strong, rather than a weak beat, and that the same is true for the final syllable in a sentence (18). He offers this sentence—"Until we know more, we cannot proceed properly"—and he then rewrites it exactly, but with the strong beats rendered in all capitals: unTIL we KNOW MORE, we canNOT proCEED PROPerly." Obviously, this sentence breaks that basic rule of syallabic rhythm. Here's how to revise to honor this idea about rhythm: "Nothing can be done until we know more." This way, the syallables that open and close the sentence are strong. Can you tell which one of these two that I've adapted from Harris is better?

> Across Kentucky that spring, the rain grew heavier and heavier.

> Everywhere in Kentucky that spring, the rains grew worse.
> (Note: if this point about rain in Kentucky is not relatively important in the larger context of the paper, you might choose to write in the less emphatic way.)

In addition to this basic concept of emphasis, ***here are several devices*** you can use to make sure your readers experience your sentences the way you want them to—that is, with the most important words in the positions of greatest emphasis. After explaining these devices for organizing rhythm within particular sentences, I'll offer some that will help you emphasize an entire sentence, as a whole, as more important than the sentences that surround it.

Climax—When a sentence offers a list, the items on that list should be arranged in order of increasing importance. This is called climax. Consider this pair of sentences and ask yourself which one uses a climax intelligently and which one, in failing to use climax, sounds absurd:

> When I lost control of the car, it careened over the curb, ran over two park benches, killed a child, and hit a water fountain.

> When I lost control of the car, it careened over a curb, ran over two park benches, hit a water fountain, and killed a child.

Can you tell which one uses the stylistic device of climax? Can you see, in this instance, how apparently minor stylistic choices actually carry with them profound ethical implications that significantly impact your readers' willingness to trust you?

Asyndeton—When you omit conjunctions between words, phrases, or clauses, you have an asyndeton, and this device helps to create a feeling of spontaneous overflow and rich abundance. Consider this pair of examples I've adapted from Harris (12):

> When he came home from World War II, the government held a grand ceremony, decorating him with medals, ribbons, titles, riches.

> When he came home from World War II, the government held a grand ceremony and decorated him with medals, ribbons, titles, and riches.

The difference is subtle, but distinct. Can you tell which one creates a mood of excess and which one a mood of relative restraint? In the context of a larger passage of prose, you can use this device to add to the mood you're trying to create, pushing toward a feeling of abundance and excitement or, if you avoid the asyndeton, one of comparative solemnity and calm reserve. Again, when you're making an argument, you'll want to create a mood or emotional energy that is appropriate to your message. Sometimes, you'll want to foster a feeling of excitement, sometimes the opposite, and these differences depend, in part, on whether or not you use the device of asyndeton.

Polysyndeton—This the opposite of asyndeton. Instead of omitting conjunctions, you use them at every available opportunity to create a slow, thudding emphasis on each of the items you're connecting. Look at the difference between these two:

> When the police opened the trunk of her car, they found stolen jewerly, loaded guns, high-grade cocaine, suitcases full of thousands of dollars.

> When the police opened the trunk of her car, they found stolen jewelry and loaded guns and high-grade cocaine and suitcases full of thousands of dollars.

Notice how one of these sentences emphasizes the individual items that were in the trunk, whereas the other sentence emphasizes the collection as a whole. Obviously, you should use polysyndeton when you want to single out each particular item in a series for particular attention, but you should use asyndeton when you aren't as concerned with the details and want to emphasize, instead, just the group as a whole with a feeling of abundance or overflow.

Expletive—An expletive is a relatively meaningless word or phrase that writers use to stop the forward momentum of a sentence and thereby give special, emphatic thrust to the words or phrases that are next to the expletive. Consider this pair of sentences from Harris:

> The lake was not drained in April.

> The lake was not, in fact, drained in April.

By using "in fact" in the second one, the words on either side of "in fact" pick up special weight, as if this writer is explicitly arguing with someone who claims that the lake actually *was* drained in April. Here's another pair:

> Many of the customers demanded a refund.

> Many of the customers, however, demanded a refund.

Can you see how one of these creates a special rhythmic thrust around "many customers / demanded," which implies that these customers differ from some other customers who don't demand refunds? Expletives are extremely useful when you want to contrast one thing with another by putting a special sort of accent on one of them, and, as such, they serve especially well when you're writing an argument. They lend emphatic force to the distinction you're making. Here are a bunch of expletives: *after all, anyway, as I said, assuredly, generally, I hope, I suppose, naturally, obviously, indeed, moreover, importantly.*

Epanelepsis—This device repeats the first word of the sentence at the end of the sentence, as in "Water was the cause of this war, yes, mere water" or "My ears heard it, but, honestly, I could not believe my ears" or "A strange looking man was standing by the side of the road as I drove to work this morning, and this afternoon, as I was driving home, I saw, in the same spot, the same strange looking man." This sort of repetition creates emphasis and draws attention to itself, so only use it when you're sure it feels appropriate.

Epixeuxis—This device repeats one word several times, as in "Louisiana in the spring is lush, lush, lush," or "That poor soul is in trouble, trouble, trouble." This device can help you create a sense of emphasis.

Irony—To make an entire sentence more emphatic, you can write it in a way that has two meanings: one that is perfectly sensible in itself and another that, in the surrounding context, is completely absurd. Here is an example I've adapted from Harris: "When the tow truck driver arrived and saw the man standing in the rain, his clothes soaked, his shoes caked in mud, his face and hands covered with grease, his car issuing giant clouds of black smoke, he heard the man mumble, 'So, I guess this means that my lovely evening is winding down.'" On one hand, there's nothing absurd about observing the end of a lovely evening, but when the surrounding context tells us that the evening could not possibly have been lovely, the man's statement becomes highly ironic. This sort of sarcasm disrupts the surface logic of your paper and draws special attention to itself, so only use this heavy emphasis when its appropriate. Misplaced sarcasm will confuse your readers and turn them off.

Understatement—This device is a particular sort of irony. Simply enough, understatement is when you deliberately articulate an idea as far less important than it is. In a sense, it is a deliberate violation of the principle of emphasis, but, in reversing emphasis, it actually creates a certain humorous sort of emphasis: "After having been lost in the desert for forty days, the two men finally stumbled in town, and one said to the other, 'You know, I feel like a cold beer, how about you?'" Again, this sort of sarcasm or irony draws considerable attention to itself, so use it wisely. Misplaced sarcasm, as I said, confuses.

Hyperbole—This device, another sort of irony, is the opposite of understatement. Hyperbole means exaggeration. Here is Harris' example: "Waiter, I told you I wanted my steak rare, not raw—I've seen cows who have been hurt worse than this just get up and walk away without demanding an apology!!!" (26). Again, be careful with this sort of irony, especially when you're making an argument, for many readers will think that you're overstating your case to conceal its essential flimsiness. In that example above, the man is probably using the hyperbole to distract from the fact that the amount of time the steak really needs on the grill is so tiny that the waiter might otherwise ignore him. While hyperbole is great for grabbing your reader's attention, it can get you into trouble with the reader if presented as completely serious and devoid of irony. Only use hyperbole if it fits within the tone of the larger essay, and only when its ironic quality is obvious.

Adianoeta—A clever but difficult device that is much like a double-entendre, in which a sentence has one meaning on the surface, but another—even opposite—meaning beneath the surface. Example: "Because the jury found him guilty and sent him to the state penitentiary, he will spend the next ten years as a special guest of the governor."

Litotes—This device for drawing attention to a sentence is also known as the "not un-" construction, as in "This movie was not unlike the one we saw last week" or "The meal I ate in the French Quarter with you was not inexpensive." While slightly awkward and unnecessarily wordy, this device, if used carefully, can call attention to itself and thereby help you to emphasize a sentence and make it stand out from the surrounding sentences. Don't use this device with sentences that aren't important enough to warrant this sort of special emphasis.

Rhetorical Question—When you ask a question that has an obvious answer, you pull your reader into a certain level of agreement with you. Here is an example from Harris: "Should this business continue with programs that have lost money two years in a row and will likely lose even more money next year?" (139). The answer is obviously no, but by asking the question anyway, a certain dramatic flair pulls the reader closer to your position. This device is very useful when you are developing an argument, for it brings a powerful emphasis to an assertion.

Aporia—This device, as Harris explains, expresses doubt about a fact, opinion, idea, or conclusion, and he offers as an example, "the question of whether or not schools should enforce dress codes is very tricky: on one hand, dress codes make gang insignia, class affiliation, and conspicuous consumption impossible, but on the other hand they enforce a drab sameness that suppresses individuality and personal tastes" (141). This device is great for introducing an argument, for showing that we need to examine certain matters more deeply. On the other hand, it is also a great way to conclude a discussion that you do not want to continue. Either way, the aporia is useful for emphasizing your key assertions.

Anantapodoton—This device leaves the second half of parallel construction unstated but implied, as in: "If you kill the alligator and eat it, you will have become a man, but if the alligator kills and eats you, well then. . . ." This sort of omission creates a powerful emphasis, so use it carefully.

Balance

Have you ever noticed how easy it is to remember certain famous sentences? Nobody ever has to sit down and memorize sentences like, "We have nothing to fear but fear itself" or "Ask not what your country can do for you but what you can do for your country." Almost like musical jingles from TV commercials, they stick. What makes these sorts of sentences stick is simply their extraordinary degree of balance. ***Here are a few devices*** to help you balance your sentences:

Parallelism—When ideas of equal importance are put in identical grammatical structures or ordered or phrased similarly, you have a parallelism. Here is an example from Harris: "To write carefully and to think clearly are interrelated goals" (1). Notice how different the effect of the sentence if you take away the parallelism: "To write carefully and clear thinking are interrelated goals." Here is another pair of sentences:

Julie likes playing the saxophone more than homework.

Julie likes playing the saxophone more than doing homework.

The difference is subtle, but one of them has a balanced rhythm that the other lacks. Can you tell which one? Though the difference might seem minor in these short sentences, the difference becomes more and more powerful in longer sentences, especially in the context of a great many sentences in a long paper.

Chiasmus—This is a fancier, more complex version of parallelism. In chiasmus, the elements that are to be balanced with one another are put in reverse order. For example, here is a parallelism from Harris: "The committee worked constantly but succeeded rarely" (5). And here is the same parallelism turned into a chiasmus: "The committee worked constantly but rarely succeeded." Do you see the difference? In the first one, a verb is followed by an adverb (worked / constantly) and then another verb is followed by another adverb (rarely / succeeded). But the second example is a chiasmus because the verb-adverb pattern isn't simply repeated but reversed: worked / constantly is followed by rarely / succeeded. Though the chiasmus might not seem like an important or powerful extension of the parallelism in these small examples, increasingly elaborate uses of chiasmus can be enormously powerful, as we'll see in the next device.

Antimetabole—This device is an elaborate version of the chiasmus, though it requires even more cleverness. It requires the second half of the sentence to repeat the first half but in reverse order, as in these examples from Harris: "Alison's job is to find a location suitable for the wedding, and Robin's job is to design a wedding suitable for the location." Or, "Instead of increasing publicity to boost our sales, we should boost our sales to increase publicity" (122). Here is a very famous antimetabole: "Ask not what your country can do for you, but what you can do for your country." When you can achieve balance at this level, you create a sentence that people will instantly remember. This sort of writing is, of course, extremely persuasive and powerful, so you certainly don't want to frame a minor, trivial point in your paper this way; instead, save these sorts of fireworks for your most important assertions.

Antithesis—When you place two terms closely together in a parallel structure to make their contrast as striking as possible, you have an antithesis. This is a great device for clarifying differences or conflicts that, otherwise, might be too complicated for the reader to engage. Consider these examples I've adapted from Harris:

> If we try, we might succeed, but if we do not put forth some effort, we'll never know whether or not we really had a chance.

> If we try, we might succeed, but if we don't, we can't. (8)

This is an especially useful device when you're developing an argument, for it allows you to contrast your own position to that of your opponent quite forcefully. Here are a few more pairs of sentences—can you tell which ones have been stylized with an antithesis and which ones haven't?

> After we parachuted out of the airplane, Lashonda said she felt completely thrilled, but my feeling was a very different one—I was still consumed with pure terror.

> After we parachuted out of the airplane, Lashonda felt thrilled and I felt terrified.

> The blueprint calls for a wall that is thick and strong, but it also says that the wall can't be very heavy because we have to be able to move it around.

> The blueprint calls for a wall that is thick and strong but also light and moveable.

Antanagoge—This device points out a fault, but balances it with a positive quality. Example: "The car sounds terrible, but it runs well."

Dirimens Copulatio—The "not only X, but also Y" construction. It is much like antanagoge, but instead of balancing positive and negative, it simply adds positive to positive or negative to negative. Example: "This book is not only hard to read, but also impossible to enjoy." "That dog is not only extremely intelligent, but also intensely loyal."

Isocolon—This device strings together phrases of nearly identical length. Example: "The movie was good—serious but never merely pretentious, funny but never merely vulgar, strange but never merely weird."

Disjunctive Proposition—This device offers two propositions, closely related, one of which must be true and the other of which must be false. Here is an example from Richard Lanham, "Either his car broke down or he forgot our appointment" (57).

Syncresis—This device, says Richard Lanham, offers a contrast in parallel clauses (147). "The purpose of living is not to live long, but to live well." Or, "A coward dies a thousand deaths. A hero dies but once."

Figurative Language

Whenever writers must explain something to a reader that the reader may find unfamiliar, the writer naturally tries to associate that unfamiliar thing with something more familiar. For example, "Because I used too much fertilizer on the palm tree, the leaves began to look like strips of bacon." There are many types of devices for adding figures to your prose, but be extremely careful to avoid figures that have been used too often. Never say, "free as a bird" or "slept like a log" or "happy as a clam." If you do, your reader will feel that your prose is dead as a doornail or flat as pancake, like this sentence is. ***Here are some devices*** for making your prose more figurative:

Simile—This device is quite simple, quite common, almost unconscious. In simile, an unfamiliar thing is explained or clarified by being associated with a more familiar thing. Importantly, the image in the simile should be quite familiar, and the subject of the simile should be something that is unclear enough to require this sort of anchoring image. For example, "I always tell my first year medical students to think of the presence of monosodium triglycerides in the bloodstream as something like a bad hair day for their heart." Notice how awful it would be to say, "A bad hair day is like having monosodium tryglycerides in your bloodstream." In this latter example, the subject is too familiar to really need any explanation, and the image that is supposed to explain it is too unfamiliar and obscure to explain much of anything to those who aren't already specialists in the subject of the bloodstream and its health. One more rule: the difference between the subject and the image should be substantial. In this example—"This particular kind of grass is as green as a grasshopper"—the simile is weak, because grasshoppers are usually the same color as grass. On the other hand, if the subject and the image are wildly different, you might need to fill in a little explanation.

Analogy—This device is just like a simile, only more elaborate. Usually, it offers several points of connection between its subject and its image, and it is explicitly designed not simply to provide a certain imaginative richness to your prose but also real conceptual clarity. As such, analogies are especially useful when dealing with abstract concepts, but, when you're developing an argument, be very careful that the links in your analogy aren't simply trying to take the place of strict logic. Here is Harris' example of a faulty analogy:

> We should get rid of all those old books in the library. After all, you don't keep worn out socks in your dresser drawer. You get rid of them!

Obviously, this analogy suffers from faulty logic, for socks are very different from books in their purpose. Also, just because the books are old doesn't mean they are worn out. Here is Harris' example of a stronger anology:

> Flash memory chips work like a chalkboard, in that, when information is written on one, the information remains present even when the power is turned off. Only when the information is deliberately erased will it disappear. And, like the chalkboard, the memory chip can be written on and erased an unlimited number of times.

Metaphor—This device also compares two different things, but goes a step further to actually identify one thing with another. For example, "My mind is barren soil" or "That man is a monster" or "Lake Pontchartrain is not a giant garbage can, and people who treat it that way are themselves nothing but trash!" "I love listening to WWOZ when I first wake up—those jazz programs are my morning coffee." In other words, a metaphor is very much like a simile, the only difference being that the metaphor does not use a "like" or an "as" between the subject and the image.

Here are some more important tips when using metaphors: first, make sure the image is something greater or more important than the subject, for if the subject is greater, the metaphor risks trivializing the subject. For example, "The waterfall poured tears upon the rock."

Obviously, tears are much tinier that what usually falls from a waterfall, and so the metaphor seems ridiculous. Notice how much better this sounds, "When she heard about the tragedy, her eyes became waterfalls." Also, if you're worried that your metaphor might seem overly strong, even distracting for your reader, you can soften it by adding an adjective: "I got caught in the thunderstorm for an hour, and my beautiful new necktie hung pitifully across my chest, a drowned snake." Notice how, if I didn't have the word "drowned" before the word snake, the sentence seems only bizarre rather than precise: "After I got caught in the thunderstorm for an hour, my beautiful new necktie hung pitifully across my chest, a snake." Putting in the word "drowned" has a way of grounding the image in the earlier information of the sentence that makes the metaphor much more effective—and much less weird.

Metonymy—This device is a version of metaphor. It doesn't simply identify one thing with another, but actually substitutes one thing for another. For example, instead of saying, "In any war, propaganda is more important than military equipment," Harris suggests you might use metonymy to say, "In any war, the pen is mightier than the sword" (63). Instead of saying, "You have to work hard every day in order to earn enough money for your meals," you might use a metonymy to say, "You have to sweat for your bread." Notice how metonymy is highly visual and very concise. That is the key to its power. Here are a few more examples: "The orders came from the White House" or "You cannot fight City Hall."

Synecdoche—This device is also a version of metaphor and is very similar to metonymy. In this case, a particular part of some whole is substituted for the whole itself. Here is an example I've adapted from Harris: "If I could save a buck, I'd buy some wheels, put on my best threads, take Jane for a ride in the moonlight, and ask for her hand" (65). In this example, "buck" subs for money, "wheels" for car, "threads" for clothing, and "hand" (in marriage) for Jane's whole person. Here is another example: "The bosses have got our blood on their hands!" Because the synechdoche is so closely associated with a certain "hipster" slang and with political slogans, be careful how you use it: if it isn't appropriate to your overall tone, avoid it.

Personification—This device metaphorically gives human attributes to things that are not human. For example, "My old car began to groan and protest as it struggled up the hill." "This computer is not very friendly." "This coffee is so strong it could pour *me* into a cup and start drinking."

Allusion—This device simply makes reference to a famous person to emphasize or add a little flash to your point. For example, "You should always remember to plan ahead—Noah couldn't have built his ark in the middle of the flood!" "If you want to play the saxophone the way John Coltrane did, you have to practice the way John Coltrane did." (Notice, in this latter example, the use of parallelism.)

Eponym—This is a particular sort of allusion, one in which the particular quality of a famous person is implied simply by the mention of that person's name. "She does so well in her math classes—I swear, she is the Michael Jordan of math." "That guy thinks he's Casanova, but none of the women can actually stand to be around him." "Up until now, that politician was nothing less than a Houdini, but the forces of justice have finally closed in on him and there's no way he can escape."

Apostrophe—This device is a direct address to someone, whether real or imaginary or personified. It serves as a dramatic outlet for pent-up emotion. For example, in an essay about movies, let's say, when the writer is describing how he watches movies every night to take his mind off his loneliness, the writer might say, "O, movies, you are my only friends!" This dramatic, abrupt switch to the second person ("you," as the focus, instead of "I") will certainly draw attention to itself and so you should use this special sort of emphasis only when appropriate—at the end of an essay, or at the end of a particularly poignant stretch of argument.

Syntax

This is the category that involves how words are arranged or sequenced. Obviously, your writing is best when it is arranged or sequenced in ways that maximize the clarity and the efficiency of your message. **Here are several devices** that involve matters of syntax.

Zeugma—There are many forms of zeugma, and they all involve linking two or more words, phrases, or clauses by another word that is stated in one place and only implied in the rest of the sentence. The simplest example is the use of one verb to serve two subjects: "Jack and Jill went up the hill." Another very common form of zeugma is in the following sentence, which has one subject but several direct objects: "She grabbed her purse from the closet in the front hall, her gloves from the table near the front door, and her car keys from the hook where she always hangs them."

Diazeugma—This is a version of the above, in which you have a single subject linking multiple verbs, as in, "Babe Ruth pitched two no-hitters, hit more than seven hundred home runs, and committed very few defensive errors." Here's another example, "We wept, fasted, prayed, preached, sacrificed, and finally succeeded."

Prozeugma—In this version, the linking word is usually a verb, and, after stating it once, you omit it, as in "The freshmen usually do best in Math; the sophomores, in music; the juniors, in chemistry."

Mesozeugma—In this version of zeugma, the linking word is placed near the middle of the sentence, as in "At eight o'clock, dinner and dessert will be served, then coffee and cigars." The link—"will be served"—comes in the middle of the sentence.

Hypozeugma—Here the linking word is placed after the words it links, as in, "An elephant, a giraffe, a rhinoceros, and a python all escaped from the Audubon Zoo early Sunday morning." What links this list of animals is "all escaped," and it comes after the list.

Syllepsis—This is primarily a device of wit, for it means using a linking word, usually a verb, to bring two different words, phrases, or clauses together, but in way that involves slightly different meanings of the linking word. For example, "He lost his heart in San Francisco and his shirt in Las Vegas." Here are some examples I've adapted from Harris: "On her way out the door, she grabbed a jacket and a kiss." "Because her date had drunk eleven beers, she decided to catch a ride home with someone else—she didn't want to risk her life or her reputation" (88).

Hyperbaton—This syntactic device, says Harris, describes any deviation from normal word order, as in "Books they have demanded and books they shall get!" or "Disturb me not!" (93). This sort of syntactical flip-flop always draws attention to itself and creates an effect of strong emphasis.

Anastrope—This transposition of words usually involves putting an adjective after the noun it modifies, as in these examples adapted from Harris (95): "She had a personality indescribable by words appropriate for polite company" or "His was a countenance sad." Or, "It was a long, difficult operation, but successful." Or, "She displayed an air of confidence unusual for one so young." Be careful with this device, for it can create some very awkward sentences. It seems to work best when the adjective is actually a long adjectival phrase, as in that last example, "unusual for one so young."

Appositive—This device is simply the use of a noun to modify or describe another noun, as in these examples from Harris: "Mr. Wilkins, the manager, saw the suspect fleeing the store with his gun drawn" or "The ability to evaluate gem stones, a skill requiring experience, knowledge, and ethics, cannot be learned overnight from a textbook." In the first example, "the manager" is a noun that modifies another noun, "Mr. Wilkins." In the second example, "a skill . . ." is a noun that modifies the earlier noun, "The ability."

Disjunctio—This device, says Richard Lanham, uses different verbs to express similar actions of one subject in successive clauses (57). Example: "By the Roman people, Cypress was destroyed, Carthage razed, Corinth burned, and Sicily overrun." Or, "This summer, her band recorded a best-selling album, drew sell-out crowds all over Europe, gave twenty-nine interviews to national magazines in the U. S., and then started its own record label."

Epiplexis—Asking a series of questions, not to gather information, but to attack. Example: "How long do you intend to test my patience? How long do you think you can get away with this? Do you want me to explode?"

Restatement

On one hand, your readers will be very turned off by your writing if they find themselves reading some particular point more than once. They'll feel that you must not have much to say if you have to keep saying the same thing over and over. Similarly, if you keep using the same words, the reader will begin to feel that those words are stale, even increasingly useless in your efforts to communicate. On the other hand, certain forms of repetition, if used strategically, can serve you quite well in connecting with your reader. ***Here are some devices*** that will allow you to repeat yourself in a way that helps rather than hinders your efforts to connect with readers:

Anaphora—This device repeats the same words at the beginning of successive clauses or sentences. Example: "They kept walking, not knowing if the mugger was still pointing the gun at them, not knowing whether they might soon die, not knowing where to contact the police." This device is useful for creating an emotionally charged mood.

Epistrophe—This device is the opposite of anaphora, for here the repetition of words comes at the end successive phases, clauses, or sentences, to create a slow, methodical effect, as in "In order for us to gain an understanding of the situation, the photographs must be analyzed, the intercepted email must be analyzed, the reports from human operatives on the ground in Pakistan must be analyzed. We cannot simply rush to judgment."

Symploce—This device, says Harris, combines anaphora and epistrophe, repeating words at both the beginnings and the endings of clauses or sentences, as in "It is not enough simply to install smoke detectors in every bedroom; smoke detectors must be maintained in every bedroom" (107). Here's another: "The problem was created by humans, and therefore the problem can be solved by humans."

Diacope—This is a direct repetition of a word or phrase after an intervening word or phrase, as in "They blew up the statue of Buddha, those villains! They blew up the statue of Buddha!" Or "The stock market did fairly well today—can you believe it?—the stock market did fairly well!" (Harris 2003, 119). This device is good for expressing powerful, dramatic emotions and so it is also a technique for emphasis. So emphatic is the diacope, in fact, that you should only use it when you're making the most important point in your essay. In fact, I would only use it as a final sentence in my paper, though using it elsewhere is certainly possible. Difficult but certainly possible. Incidentally, did you notice the diacope in the preceding sentence?

Accumulatio—This device heaps up terms of praise or of condemnation to summarize the points you've made. It works especially well in the conclusion of your paper. Example: "Thus, we see that the Mayor Smith has been arrogant, uninformed, disloyal, greedy, deceitful, unreliable, and destructive."

Sound

Even when readers are reading silently, tiny movements register in their vocal cords, sending subtle signals throughout the body that undoubtedly play a role in the reader's pleasure. Certain stylistic devices can capitalize directly on this potential for sound to stimulate a subtle pleasure in the reader.

Alliteration—This device works by repeating certain consonant sounds at the beginning of successive words. For example, "The late delivery of the data resulted in a disheartening delay and caused the entire department to miss the deadline for distributing their reports."

Onomontopoeia—This term refers to a word that, when pronounced, imitates the sound that the word names. For example, "Plop," "Buzz," "Fizz," "Ooze," "Slam," "Scratch," "Rattle."

Assonance—This device repeats vowels sounds, as in, "A whole boat load of tourists from Oklahoma are hoping to float down the Bogachitta River most of the day, then go back their to hotels in New Orleans to enroll for that evening's ghost tour."

Consonance—This device repeats consonant sounds at the ends of words. It's much like alliteration, therefore, only focusing on the ends of words rather than their beginnings. For example, "He gave me a helpful tip—just rip the cap off the top and, when you sip, don't cut your lip."

Works Cited

Abrams, M. H. 1953. *The Mirror and the Lamp*. New York: Oxford University Press.

Adams, Hazard. 1971. *Critical Theory Since Plato*. New York: Harcourt Brace Jovanovich.

Allen, Guy. 2000. "Language, Power, and Consciousness: A Writing Experiment at the University of Toronto." *Writing and Healing: Toward an Informed Practice*, eds. Charles Anderson and Marian MacCurdy, 249–90. Urbana, IL: National Council of Teachers of English.

Anderson, Charles, and Marian MacCurdy. 2000. Introduction to *Writing and Healing: Toward an Informed Practice*, 1–23. Urbana, IL: National Council of Teachers of English.

Bartholomae, David. 1985. "Inventing the University." *When Writers Can't Write: Studies in Writer's Block and Other Composing Process Problems*, 134–65. New York: Guilford Press.

———. 1990. "A Reply to Stephen North" *Pre/Text: A Journal of Rhetorical Theory* 11: 121–30.

———. 1995. "Writing with Teachers: A Conversation with Peter Elbow." *College Composition and Communication* 46 (1): 62–71.

Bartholomae, David, and Anthony Petrosky, eds. 1986. *Facts, Artifacts, and Counterfacts*. Portsmouth, NH: Boynton/Cook.

———. 1993. *Ways of Reading*. Boston: Bedford.

Baudrillard, Jean. 1993. *Symbolic Exchange and Death*. Trans. Iain Hamilton Grant. Thousand Oaks, CA: Sage.

Bazerman, Charles. 1992. "Theories That Help Us Write Better." In *A Rhetoric of Doing: Essays on Written Discourse in Honor of James L. Kinneavy*, eds. Stephen Witte, Neil Nakadate, and Roger Cherry. Carbondale: Southern Illinois University Press.

Benson, Thomas. 1996. "Longinus." In *Encyclopedia of Rhetoric and Composition: Communication from Ancient Times to the Information Age*, ed. Theresa Enos, 415–16. New York: Garland.

Berlin, James. 1987. *Rhetoric and Reality: Writing Instruction in American Colleges, 1900–1985*. Carbondale: Southern Illinois University Press.

Berman, Jeffrey, and Jonathan Schiff. 2000. "Writing About Suicide." *Writing and Healing: Toward an Informed Practice*, eds. Charles Anderson and

Marian MacCurdy, 291–312. Urbana, IL: National Council of Teachers of English.

Bizzell, Patricia. 1986. "What Happens When Basic Writers Come to College." *College Composition and Communication* 37 (3): 294–301.

Bizzell, Patricia, and Bruce Herzberg, eds. 1990. *The Rhetorical Tradition: Readings from Classical Times to the Present.* Boston: Bedford/St. Martin's Press.

Blitz, Michael, and C. Mark Hulbert. 1998. *Letters for the Living: Teaching Writing in a Violent Age.* Urbana, IL: National Council of Teachers of English.

Boler, Megan. 1999. *Feeling Power: Emotions and Education.* New York: Routledge.

Bourdieu, Pierre, and Jean-Claude Passerson. 1977. *Reproduction in Education, Society, and Culture.* Trans. Richard Nice. London: Sage.

Boyd, Richard. 1999. "Reading Student Resistance: The Case of the Missing Other." *Journal of Advanced Composition* 19 (4): 589–605.

Bracher, Mark. 1999. *The Talking Cure: Psychoanalysis, Composition, and the Aims of Education.* Carbondale: Southern Illinois University Press.

Brand, Alice Glarden, and Richard Graves, eds. 1994. *Presence of Mind: Writing and the Domain Beyond the Cognitive.* Portsmouth, NH: Boynton/Cook.

Brooke, Robert. 1987. "Underlife and Writing Instruction." *College Composition and Communication* 38 (2): 141–53.

Bruner, Jerome. 1962. *On Knowing: Essays for the Left Hand.* Cambridge, MA: Harvard University Press.

———. 1966. *Toward a Theory of Instruction.* Cambridge, MA: Harvard University Press.

Burke, Kenneth. 1945. *A Grammar of Motives.* Berkeley: University of California Press.

Cicero. 1970. *On Oratory and Orators.* Trans. and ed. J. S. Watson. Carbondale: Southern Illinois University Press.

Cixous, Hélène. 1990. "The Laugh of the Medusa." Trans. Keith Cohen and Paula Cohen. In *The Rhetorical Tradition: Readings from Classical Times to the Present,* eds. Patricia Bizzell and Bruce Herzberg, 1232–45. Boston: Bedford/St. Martin's Press.

Cixous, Helene, and Catherine Clement. 1986. *The Newly Borne Woman.* Trans. Betsey Wing. Minneapolis: University of Minnesota Press.

Connors, Robert. 2000. "The Erasure of the Sentence." *College Composition and Communication* 52 (1): 96–128.

Couliano, Ioan. 1987. *Eros and Magic in the Renaissance.* Trans. Margaret Cooke. Chicago: University of Chicago Press.

Covino, William. 1988. *The Art of Wondering.* Portsmouth, NH: Boynton/Cook.

———. 1994. *Magic, Literacy, Rhetoric: An Eccentric History of the Composing Imagination.* Albany: State University of New York Press.

Crowley, Sharon, and Debra Hawhee. 1999. *Ancient Rhetorics for Contemporary Students.* New York: Longman.

Davis, D. Diane. 2000. *Breaking Up (At) Totality: A Rhetoric of Laughter.* Carbondale: Southern Illinois University Press.

Delbanco, Nicholas. 2002. "In Praise of Imitation: On the Sincerest Form of Flattery." *Harper's* (July): 57–63.

Deleuze, Gilles. 1991. *Coldness and Cruelty.* New York: Zone Books.

———. 1994. *Difference and Repetition.* Trans. Paul Patton. New York: Columbia University Press.

Derksen, Daniel John, and Victor C. Strasburger. 1996. "Media and Television Violence: Effects on Violence, Aggression, and Antisocial Behavior in Children." In *Schools, Violence, and Society,* ed. Allan M. Hoffman, 61–78. Westport, CT: Praeger.

De Romilly, Jacqueline. 1992. *The Great Sophists of Periclean Athens.* Trans. Janet Lloyd. Oxford: Oxford University Press.

Dewey, John. 1994. *Democracy in Education.* New York: The Free Press.

Dilks, Stephen, Regina Hansen, and Matthew Parfitt. 2001. *Cultural Conversations: The Presence of the Past.* Boston: Bedford/St. Martin's Press.

Dodds, E. R. 1951. *The Greeks and the Irrational.* Berkeley: University of California Press.

Dubois, Page. 1991. *Torture and Truth.* New York: Routledge.

Eaves, Morris. 1982. *William Blake's Theory of Art.* Princeton, NJ: Princeton University Press.

Edmundson, Mark. 1997. "On the Uses of a Liberal Education." *Harper's* (September): 39–49.

Elbow, Peter. 1973. *Writing Without Teachers.* Oxford: Oxford University Press.

———. 1981. *Writing with Power: Techniques for Mastering the Writing Process.* New York: Oxford University Press.

———. 1985/1999. "The Shifting Relationships Between Speech and Writing." In *The Braddock Essays, 1975–1998,* ed. Lisa Ede. Boston: Bedford/St. Martin's Press.

Entralgo, Pedro Lain. 1970. *The Therapy of the Word in Classical Antiquity.* Trans. L. J. Rather and Jon Sharp. New Haven, CT: Yale University Press.

Faigley, Lester. 1986. "Competing Theories of Process: A Critique and a Proposal." *College English* 48 (6): 527–39.

Felman, Shoshana. 1997. "Psychoanalysis and Education: Pedagogy Terminable and Interminable." In *Learning Desire: Perspectives on Pedagogy, Culture, and the Unsaid,* ed. Sharon Todd, 17–44. New York: Routledge.

Ficino, Marsilio. 1989. *Three Books on Life.* Trans. Carol Caske and John Clark. Binghamton, NY: Medieval and Renaissance Texts in Conjunction with the Renaissance Society of America.

Freud, Sigmund. 1933/1964. *The Complete Psychological Works of Sigmund Freud,* Vol. XXII. Trans. and ed. James Strachey. London: Hogarth Press.

Fulkerson, Richard. 1998. "Call Me Horatio: Negotiating Between Cognition and Affect in Composition." *College Composition and Communication* 50 (1): 101–15.

Gallop, Jane. 1997. *Feminist Accused of Sexual Harrassment*. Durham, NC: Duke University Press.

Gery, John. 1999. "Sense and Unsense." In *Teaching Composition with Literature: 101 Writing Assignments from College Instructors*, eds. Dana Gioia and Patricia Wagner, 158–60. New York: Longman.

Gorgias. 1977. "On Nature, or The Non-Existent." In *Ancilla to the Pre-Socratic Philosophers*. Trans. and ed. Kathleen Freeman. Cambridge, MA: Harvard University Press.

———. 1990. "Encomium of Helene." Trans. Rosamond Kent Sprague. In *The Rhetorical Tradition: Readings from Classical Times to the Present*, eds. Patricia Bizzell and Bruce Herzberg. Boston: Bedford/St. Martin's Press.

Gradin, Sherrie L. 1995. *Romancing Rhetorics: Social-Expressivist Perspectives on the Teaching of Writing*. Portsmouth, NH: Boynton/Cook.

Harris, Joseph. 1996. *A Teaching Subject: Composition Since 1966*. Upper Saddle River, NJ: Prentice-Hall.

Harris, Robert. 2003. *Writing with Clarity and Style*. Los Angeles: Pyrczak Publishing.

Havelock, Eric. 1963. *Preface to Plato*. Oxford: Blackwell.

Hawkins, Anne Hunsaker. 2000. "Pathography and Enabling Myths: The Process of Healing." In *Writing and Healing: Toward an Informed Practice*, eds. Charles Anderson and Marian MacCurdy, 222–47. Urbana, IL: National Council of Teachers of English.

Helmers, Marguerite H. 1994. *Writing Students: Composition Testimonials and Representations of Students*. Albany: State University of New York Press.

Herman, Judith. 1992. *Trauma and Recovery*. New York: Basic.

hooks, bell. 2000. "Rhapsody Remembered: Dancing with Words." *Journal of Advanced Composition* 20 (1): 1–8.

Horner, Bruce. 2000. "Traditions and Professionalization: Reconceiving Work in Composition." *College Composition and Communication* 51 (3): 366–96.

Horner, Bruce, and Min-Zhan Lu. 1998. "The Problematic of Experience: Redefining Critical Work in Ethnography and Pedagogy." *College English* 60 (3): 257–77.

Iser, Wolfgang. 1978. *The Act of Reading: A Theory of Aesthetic Response*. Baltimore: Johns Hopkins University Press.

Jarratt, Susan. 1998. *Rereading the Sophists: Classical Rhetoric Refigured*. Carbondale: Southern Illinois University Press.

Johnson, Mark. 1987. *The Body in the Mind*. Chicago: University of Chicago Press.

Johnson, T. R. 1998. "An Apology for Pleasure, or Rethinking Romanticism and the Student Writer." *Composition Studies* 26 (2): 35–58.

Katz, Stephen. 1996. *The Epistemic Music of Rhetoric*. Carbondale: Southern Illinois University Press.

Kennedy, George. 1999. *Classical Rhetoric and Its Christian and Secular Tradition from Ancient to Modern Times*. Chapel Hill: University of North Carolina Press.

Kinneavy, James. 1986. "Kairos: A Neglected Concept in Classical Rhetoric." In *Rhetoric and Praxis,* ed. Jean Dietz Moss. Washington, DC: Catholic University of America Press.

Lacan, Jacques. 1991a. *The Seminar of Jacques Lacan, Book I: Freud's Papers on Technique, 1953–1954.* Trans. John Forrester and ed. Jacques-Alain Miller. New York: Norton.

———. 1991b. *The Seminar of Jacques Lacan, Book II: The Ego in Freud's Theory and in the Technique of Psychoanalysis, 1954–1955.* Trans. Sylvia Tomaselli and ed. Jacques-Alain Miller. New York: Norton.

Lanham, Richard. 1974. *Style: An Anti-Textbook.* New Haven, CT: Yale University Press.

———. 1983. *Analyzing Prose.* New York: Scribner's.

———. 1991. *A Handlist of Rhetorical Terms.* Berkeley: University of California Press.

Laplanche, J., and J. B. Pontalis. 1973. *The Language of Psychoanalysis.* New York: Norton.

Lees, Elaine O. 1987. "Proofreading as Reading, Error as Embarrassment." In *A Sourcebook for Basic Writing Teachers,* ed. Theresa Enos. New York: Random House.

Lloyd-Jones, Richard. 1970. "Theoretical Problems with Studying Creativity in Composition." *College Composition and Communication* 21 (3): 262–68.

Longinus. 1971. "On the Sublime." In *Critical Theory Since Plato,* ed. Hazard Adams. New York: Harcourt Brace Jovanovich.

MacCurdy, Marian. 2000. "From Trauma to Writing: A Theoretical Model for Practical Use." In *Writing and Healing: Toward an Informed Practice,* eds. Charles Anderson and Marian MacCurdy. Urbana, IL: National Council of Teachers of English.

Mandel, Barrett. 1980. "The Writer Writing Is Not at Home." *College Composition and Communication* 31: 371–77.

Mandler, Jean. 1991. "How to Build a Baby: II. Conceptual Primitives" *Psychological Review*: 587–604.

McGann, Jerome. 1973. "The Aims of Blake's Prophecies and the Uses of Blake Criticism." In *Blake's Sublime Allegory,* eds. Stuart Curran and Joseph Antony Wiettreich, 3–22. Madison: University of Wisconsin Press.

McLeod, Susan. 1997. *Notes on the Heart: Affective Issues in the Writing Classroom.* Carbondale: Southern Illinois University Press.

Miller, Hildy. 1994. "Sites of Inspiration: Where Writing Is Embodied in Image and Emotion." In *Presence of Mind: Writing and the Domain Beyond the Cognitive,* eds. Alice Glarden Brand and Richard Graves. Portsmouth, NH: Boynton/Cook.

Miller, J. Hillis. 1983. "Composition and Decomposition: Deconstruction and the Teaching of Writing." In *Composition and Literature: Bridging the Gap,* ed. Winifred Horner, 38–56. Chicago: University of Chicago Press.

Miller, Richard. 1996. "The Nervous System." *College English* 58 (3): 265–85.

Miller, Susan. 1991. *Textual Carnivals: The Politics of Composition.* Carbondale: Southern Illinois University Press.

Mitchell, W. J. T. 1973. "Blake's Radical Comedy: Dramatic Structures as Meaning in Blake's 'Milton.'" In *Blake's Sublime Allegory,* eds. Stuart Curran and Joseph Antony Wiettreich, 281–308. Madison: University of Wisconsin Press.

Murphy, Ann. 1989. "Transference and Resistance in the Basic Writing Classroom." *College Composition and Communication* 40 (2): 175–87.

Murray, Donald. 1972/1997. "Teach Writing as a Process, Not a Product." In *Cross-Talk in Comp Theory,* ed. Victor Villanueva. Urbana, IL: National Council of Teachers of English.

———. 1982. "Teaching the Other Self: The Writer's First Reader." *College Composition and Communication* 23 (2): 140–46.

Neel, Jasper. 1988. *Plato, Derrida, and Writing.* Carbondale: Southern Illinois University Press.

Nussbaum, Martha. 1994. *The Therapy of Desire: Theory and Practice in Hellenistic Ethics.* Princeton, NJ: Princeton University Press.

O'Keefe, Daniel Lawrence. 1982. *Stolen Lightning: The Social Theory of Magic.* New York: Continuum.

Ong, Walter. 1971. *Rhetoric, Romance, Technology.* Ithaca, NY: Cornell University Press.

———. 1975/1997. "The Writer's Audience Is Always a Fiction." In *Cross-Talk in Comp Theory,* ed. Victor Villanueva. Urbana, IL: National Council of Teachers of English.

———. 1982. *Orality and Literacy.* New York: Methuen.

Payne, Michelle. 2000. "A Strange, Unaccountable Something: Historicizing Sexual Abuse Essays." In *Writing and Healing: Toward an Informed Practice,* eds. Charles Anderson and Marian MacCurdy, 115–57. Urbana, IL: National Council of Teachers of English.

Perl, Sondra. 1979. "The Composing Process of Unskilled Writers." *Research in the Teaching of English* 13: 317–36.

———. 1980. "Understanding Composing." *College Composition and Communication* 31 (4): 363–69.

———. 1994. "A Writer's Way of Knowing: Guidelines for Composing." In *Presence of Mind: Writing and the Domain Beyond the Cognitive,* eds. Alice Glarden Brand and Richard Graves, 77–88. Portsmouth, NH: Boynton/Cook.

Rodriguez, Richard. 1993. "The Achievement of Desire." In *Ways of Reading,* eds. David Bartholomae and Anthony Petrosky, 481–504. Boston: Bedford.

Rogers, Carl. 1961. *On Becoming a Person: A Therapist's View of Therapy.* Boston: Houghton Mifflin.

———. 1969. *Freedom to Learn*. Columbus, OH: Merrill.

Rorty, Richard. 1991. "Science as Solidarity." In *Objectivity, Relativism, Truth*, 35–45. Cambridge, England: Cambridge University Press.

Rose, Mike. 1980. "Rigid Rules, Inflexible Plans, and the Stifling of Language: A Cognitivist Analysis of Writer's Block." *College Composition and Communication* 31 (4): 389–400.

Roskelly, Hephzibah, and Kate Ronald. 1998. *Reason to Believe: Romanticism, Pragmatism, and the Teaching of Writing*. Albany: State University of New York Press.

Runicman, Lex. 1991. "Fun?" *College English* 53 (2): 156–62.

Scarry, Elaine. 1985. *The Body in Pain: The Making and Unmaking of the World*. New York: Oxford University Press.

Schneiderman, Stuart. 1983. *Jacques Lacan: The Death of an Intellectual Hero*. Cambridge, MA: Harvard University Press.

Schreiner, Steven. 1997. "A Portrait of the Writer as a Young Student: Re-evaluating Emig and the Process Movement." *College Composition and Communication* 48 (1): 86–104.

Segal, George. 1962. "Gorgias and the Psychology of Logos." *Harvard Studies in Classical Philology* 66: 99–155.

Sick: The Life and Death of Bob Flanagan, Super-Masochist. 1997. Dir. Kirby Dick. Perf. Bob Flanagan, Sheree Rose.

Sirc, Geoffrey. 2002. *English Composition as a Happening*. Logan: Utah State University Press.

Stuckey, J. Eslpeth. 1991. *The Violence of Literacy*. Portsmouth, NH: Boynton/Cook.

Sullivan, Henry. 2002. Conversation with the author.

Taylor, Anya. 1979. *Magic and English Romanticism*. Athens: University of Georgia Press.

Vitanza, Victor. 1997. *Negation, Subjectivity, and the History of Rhetoric*. Albany: State University of New York Press.

Vopat, James. 1978. "Uptaught Rethought." *College English* 40 (1): 41–45.

Welch, Nancy. 1997. *Getting Restless: Rethinking Revision in Writing Instruction*. Portsmouth, NH: Boynton/Cook.

Williams, Joseph. 1981. "The Phenomenology of Error." *College Composition and Communication* 32 (2): 152–68.

———. 2000. *Style: Ten Lessons in Clarity and Grace*. New York: Longman.

Williams, Raymond. 1977. *Marxism and Literature*. New York: Oxford University Press.

Worsham, Lynn. 1991. "Writing Against Writing: The Predicament of Écriture Feminine in Composition Studies." In *Contending with Words: Composition and Rhetoric in a Postmodern Age*, eds. Patricia Harkin and John Schilb, 82–104. New York: Modern Language Association.

————. 1993. "Emotion and Pedagogic Violence" *Discourse* 15 (2): 119–49.

————. 1998. "Going Postal: Pedagogic Violence and the Schooling of Emotion." *Journal of Advanced Composition:* 214–45.

Young, Richard. 1982. "Concepts of Art and the Teaching of Writing." In *The Rhetorical Tradition in Modern Writing,* ed. James J. Murphy: New York: Modern Language Association.

Zizek, Slavoj. 1989. *The Sublime Object of Ideology.* London: Verso.

————. 1992. *Looking Awry: An Introduction to Jacques Lacan Through Popular Culture.* Cambridge, MA: MIT Press.

————. 2002. *The Fragile Absolute, Or, Why the Christian Legacy Is Worth Fighting For.* London: Verso.